In these tumultuous times, with increasing geopolitical turmoil, political, financial, and social issues, as well as challenging domestic situations, Tony Suárez assures us all is well. *The Triumphant Church* reflects on the history of Christianity and reveals how the church thrived in the midst of persecution and tribulation. Tony's dynamic and anointed way with words—in the pulpit and on the printed page—depicts an extraordinary future for believers. This book is a page-turner, and offers immense optimism as it illustrates our best days have not yet been experienced.

—MORTON BUSTARD, author and minister

Pastor Tony Suárez represents a remnant of men and women in his generation who have determined that they are not going to be silenced, stopped, or even slowed down in pursuit of God's presence and the advancement of kingdom purpose. I admire him for a multitude of reasons, among them his character, obedience, and faith after suffering incalculable loss. Tony remains stead-fast in the prophetic proclamation of the unsearchable riches of Christ. Unlike so many, who fear persecution and seek safety from opposition, he stands his ground while moving relentlessly forward to reclaim enemy held territory. Pastor Suárez will inspire you to join him as together we experience the victory that will always come to those who trust God regardless of the pain of their present circumstance. *The Triumphant Church* will cause you to gain a new perspective on 2 Corinthians 2:14:

"Now thanks be to God who always causes us to triumph in Christ." It will also remind you there is still a God who creates, a King who redeems, a cross that bleeds, a Spirit who fills, and a prayer that is heard and answered. And there is still a triumphant, victorious church of Jesus Christ against which the gates of hell shall not prevail.

—Dr. Rod Parsley, pastor and founder,
World Harvest Church, Columbus, Ohio

Tony Suárez is a carrier of the anointing. His revelation of the triumphant church will redirect your spirit back to your first love, and his words will redirect you to carry the marching orders of God as a triumphant army. This book will bless you!

—Pastor Myles Rutherford,
Worship with Wonders Church

The Triumphant Church will help you to be so filled with the Holy Spirit that it's impossible for those around you not to know it.

—Jentezen Franklin, senior pastor, Free Chapel,
New York Times best-selling author

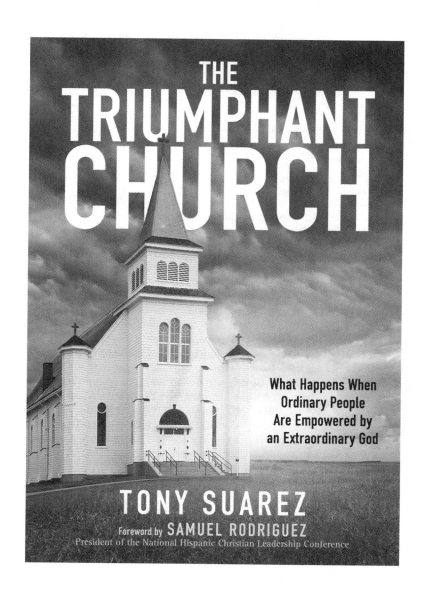

THE
TRIUMPHANT
CHURCH

What Happens When
Ordinary People
Are Empowered by
an Extraordinary God

TONY SUAREZ

Foreword by SAMUEL RODRIGUEZ
President of the National Hispanic Christian Leadership Conference

BroadStreet
P U B L I S H I N G

BroadStreet Publishing® Group, LLC
Savage, Minnesota, USA
BroadStreetPublishing.com

The Triumphant Church: What Happens When Ordinary People Are
Empowered by an Extraordinary God

Stock or custom editions of BroadStreet Publishing titles may be purchased in
bulk for educational, business, ministry, fundraising, or sales promotional use.
For information, please email info@broadstreetpublishing.com.

Cover design by Chris Garborg at garborgdesign.com
Typesetting by Kjell Garborg at garborgdesign.com

Printed in the United States of America
18 19 20 21 22 5 4 3 2 1

Dedicated to the memory of my natural and spiritual father, Rito Antonio Suárez, who taught my brother and me to never "come down off the wall," to never allow distractions to stop us from building the kingdom of God on the earth (Nehemiah 6:3), and if you're going to do something for the Lord, make sure it costs you something (1 Chronicles 21:24).

Contents

Foreword

Some argue that we are living in the darkest hour of humankind—darkened by sin, immorality, moral relativism, spiritual apathy, cultural decadence, infanticide, racism, pornography, poverty, false prophets, watered down preaching, hypocrisy, unbridled consumerism, voyeurism, materialism, secular tyranny, religious fundamentalism, discord, division, strife, hatred, jealousy, and unbelief. Yet, in the midst of darkness there stems a prophetic truth—a revealed truth, an everlasting truth—uttered by our Savior: "You are the light of the world. A city set on a hill cannot be hidden" (Matthew 5:14).

The lies of the enemies must be countered by the truth that we find in Christ. Remember, for every Pharaoh there has been a Moses. For every Goliath, there must be a David. For every Nebuchadnezzar, there must be a Daniel. For every Jezebel, there must be an Elijah. For every Herod, there must be a Jesus. And for every devil that rises up against us? There is a mightier God that rises up for us!

It is time for the church to rise up! Within our evangelical belief system, we have spent a great deal of time praying and waiting for Jesus to come down and rescue his bride. But I firmly believe that while we are waiting for Jesus to come down, he's waiting on us to rise up, as the triumphant church he ordained us to be.

We are not just another institution in society, nor are we another religious faith narrative competing in the marketplace of ideas.

We are not a piece of feel-good machinery for the spiritually impaired, nor are we an antiquated conduit for a set of irrelevant values no longer applicable in the world of Facebook, iPads, Twitter, Instagram, and YouTube.

We must respond with clarity, conviction, and courage regarding who we are:

- We are the light of the world and a city on a hill (Matthew 5:14).
- We are people of the word (1 Kings 8:56).
- We are salt and light (Matthew 5:13–16).
- We are prophetic and not pathetic.

- We are disciples, witnesses, and Christ-followers
  (Matthew 28:16–20).
- We are apostles, prophets, evangelists, pastors, and teachers
  (Ephesians 4:11).
- We are children of the cross (Romans 8:17), fruit of the empty
  tomb (John 12:24), and product of the upper room (Acts 2).
- We are the redeemed of the Lord (Psalm 107:2).
- We are the sheep of his pasture (Psalm 100:3).
- We are forgiven, free, and favored (Luke 23:24).
- We are called and chosen (1 Peter 2:9).
- We are warriors and worshipers (Psalm 144:1).
- We are world changers and history-makers (Mark 16:15).
- We are not Google, Microsoft, or Ford; we are far better.
  We are, after all, the church of Jesus Christ, and the gates of
  hell shall not, cannot, and will not prevail against us! Hallelu-
  jah! (Matthew 16:18)

To that regard, my spiritual son and younger brother, Tony
Suárez, otherwise known as Pastor Samuel Rodriguez's "Elisha," car-
ries an anointing to unleash a multi-generational commitment to this
triumphant church. Tony's personal narrative is one of perseverance,
resilience, and the supernatural power of God. His voice is prophetic, his
ministry transformative, and his calling transformational.

So I want to make this clear: To the enemies of truth, grace, hope,
and love; to those who want the oracles of righteousness and justice to
disappear; to those who would like the church to be locked in a perpetual echo chamber of affirmation on Sunday mornings; to those who
would like us to stop saying that we are created in the image of God; to
those who would like us to stop declaring that every life is sacred in the
womb and out of the womb; to those who would like us to stop preaching that there's only one way to be saved, and that way is Jesus; and to
those who would like us to stop teaching God's Word: I have news for
you. Get ready to be disappointed! For we are about to raise our volume
like never before. For we are a TRIUMPHANT CHURCH!

Dr. Samuel Rodriguez
President of the National Hispanic Christian Leadership Conference
Lead Pastor of New Season, Sacramento, CA

1

The Destiny before Us

Like most church-going kids who grew up in the baby boomer generation and Generation X, I spent most Sunday nights under a church pew. Those nights consisted of racing Hot Wheels cars, coloring, and eventually falling asleep—all while melodic hymns of praise and fiery preaching filled the sanctuary where we were gathered. As engaged as I was with life as I knew it under the pew, the sounds of singing and preaching are my most vivid memories of growing up in a Pentecostal church. Though they should have just been background noise to a young child, they captivated my attention.

One specific service has always stood out in my mind. I couldn't have been older than six years old. It was our church's annual Watchnight service, and I was determined to stay awake long enough to witness the custom of foot washing and watch as our church family celebrated communion. As with most evangelicals, especially within the charismatic and Pentecostal circles, Watchnight was always a good service. We'd celebrate all the Lord had done for us in the previous year and worship in anticipation for what he was going to do in the upcoming year. It was always one of our favorite celebrations, and a celebration it was!

I fought sleep and did everything I could to stay awake. I eventually succumbed to sleep, but not before the voice of the speaker for that evening, Pastor Rick Wyser, rang in my ears and stayed in my heart. His Scripture for the evening came from Matthew 16:18, and his voice thundered with passion, "The gates of hell shall not prevail against the church!" He said this phrase over and over and over again, "The gates of hell shall not–they cannot, and they will not–prevail against the church!" I fell asleep to those words.

More than three decades have passed since I heard those words for the first time, yet they still ring in my spirit. When I read or hear that passage, my mind goes back to that night service in Addison, Illinois, where as a child I first heard that prophetic and victorious proclamation: The gates of hell shall not prevail against the church.

I've found those words to be precisely true. The church, of which Jesus Christ is the chief cornerstone and the foundation, the door and the path, the head and groom, has stood the test of time. Hell has tried to rise against it, and it surely has gone through its vexing and trying times, yet the church still stands as a testament to the everlasting truth that what God promises, God fulfills.

Modern-Day Church

When I was growing up during the eighties, the church placed a tremendous emphasis on teaching and preaching the second coming of the Lord Jesus Christ. The emphasis went beyond teaching and preaching; it was even in our songs and featured on television programs and movies. I think anyone who grew up between the seventies and the early nineties remembers the emphasis I'm talking about. We preached about the Second Coming, we sang about the Second Coming, and we were expectant for the Second Coming. We believed that "soon and very soon," at any moment, the trumpet was going to sound, and we would meet those who had already passed away and be caught up to heaven. We were going to see the King!

Movies like *Thief in the Night* were made and literally scared people into salvation. I say this jokingly of course, but if you couldn't walk in salvation through the joy of the Lord, we were going to make sure you were saved by the fear of the Lord. It's true we should always be ready for the coming of the Lord, but there was just an extra emphasis about being ready and an understanding that you didn't want to be left behind. If you weren't living for the Lord the way you should, there was that small voice in your mind that would remind you, *Jesus is coming!* We were living in perpetual expectation that Jesus Christ was going to come back for his church at any given moment.

We were hyper-focused on evangelism lest anyone be left behind. We were intently focused on making disci-

ples and winning the lost. That focus is still at the core of
our church, but over the last decade or so a considerable
amount of introspection has occurred within the body of
Christ as to who we are. While reflection is good, it has also
caused us to become very critical of ourselves. I think we
saw—or at least we thought we saw, wrinkles and blemishes
that maybe weren't or aren't as bad as we initially perceived
them to be. But when you stare at anything long enough, it
seems to grow before your eyes. These perceived blemishes
led many leaders in the church to question the strength and
health of the church in our day. Many openly spoke against
it and cried out over the evil and lethargy that they were
convinced were widespread in the church.

Even today some are fearful of the church; they're
unsure and uncomfortable about what's going to happen in
the twenty-first century. While the baton has been passed,
it seems to have been more reluctantly handed over than
passed. Some have been anxious to let go because of their
concern over what the church may become.

I understand those concerns. There are surely things to
be concerned about, yet I also ask you, when has an older
generation not had concerns about their succeeding generation? There is a perpetual cry within the church body and
the secular society for the "old days." We become nostalgic
for what we had or how things were. While nostalgia in
itself isn't a bad thing, getting caught up over what *was*
surely is a bad thing. God's Word and truth is everlasting
and unchanging, but his methods and plans for carrying out
his message have changed with every generation.

In these last several years it seemed like it became very popular to preach messages that did nothing more than criticize the church. Many times, I would attend a conference or a special service, and I'd hear sermons begin with the phrase, "The problem with the church is ..." I heard this phrase often as the church became very inward-focused; all we could see or focus on were problems, faults, and shortcomings. While we brought most of these issues on ourselves, and we in no way condone our mistakes, the burning question that was in my mind at those times—and the question that must be asked today—was and is: When has the church *not* had problems?

What generation hasn't had their issues? The first-century church was ravaged with issues, which you'll read about later. As the centuries wore on, the church endured struggles within itself, fights, wars, persecution, and such. It seems that a portion of the church was involved in European conflicts, politics, and wars throughout much of the Medieval and Renaissance periods of history. As the church grew beyond Jerusalem and into the uttermost parts of the earth (as Jesus had said it would), growth brought conflict and even division. One church that began on the day of Pentecost would begin a pattern of splintering off and lead us to thousands of different denominations, networks, and affiliations—both within Catholicism and Protestantism.

Speaking specifically of the United States, if the 1930s to 1950s were the golden era of American Christianity, as many say it was, how do we reconcile that with our embarrassing history of racism and segregation during the same

time period? We cherish and honor the outpouring of the
Holy Spirit in Topeka, Kansas, in 1901, yet we are equally
ashamed that the future leader of the Azusa Street revival, William Seymour, was forced to learn from outside the
classroom because of the color of his skin. The church has
always had serious issues to be concerned about, yet the
gates of hell haven't prevailed.

Cause for Concern?

Respected and credible ministries from the last decade
have brought too many warnings for you and me to simply
write these concerns off as unfounded criticism. I'm sure
we have grieved the heart of God with the overemphasis
on prosperity, the disregard for spiritual accountability, the
departure from holiness. We asked God to do a supernatural
work in us, to make us debt-free, to help us build bigger
buildings, and more. And then after he did the work, some
churches relegated the Holy Spirit and his manifestations to
a back room or corner.

In an attempt to dissociate ourselves from scandals
and some of the craziness that we found within our spiritual
family, some went to the other extreme and no longer bared
a resemblance to a Spirit-empowered or a Spirit-led church.
Some within our ranks allowed themselves to go beyond
the questioning of methods, and they questioned—or even
changed—the message they once preached regarding the
Holy Spirit.

A call to repentance, a warning, and a correction are
in order. Rather than correct, however, at most we just criti-

cized and complained. It became a fad to knock the church, to prophesy our demise, and to give the appearance that we were waving the proverbial white flag. While the concern bears merit, it must be weighed against Scripture. If we believe God's Word, the increase of his government shall have no end (Isaiah 9:7), and his church will stand!

The Name of Jesus

I remember hearing Gloria Gaither recite the following words regarding our Savior. She said:

> Jesus—the mere mention of his name can calm the storm, heal the broken, and raise the dead. At the name of Jesus, I've seen sin-hardened men melted, derelicts transformed, and the light of hope put in the eyes of a hopeless child. At the name of Jesus, hatred and bitterness turn to love and forgiveness, and arguments cease. I've heard a mother softly breathe His name at the bedside of a child delirious from fever, and watched as that little body grew quiet, and that fevered brow, cool. I've sat at the bedside of a dying saint. Her body wracked with pain, who in those final, fleeting seconds summoned her last ounce of ebbing strength, just to whisper earth's sweetest name ... Jesus. Emperors have tried to

destroy it. Philosophies have tried to stamp it out. Tyrants have tried to wash it from the face of the earth with the very blood of those who claimed it. Yet it still stands. And there shall be that final day when every voice that has ever uttered a sound, every voice of Adam's race shall rise in one mighty chorus to proclaim the name Jesus. For in that day, every knee shall bow, and every tongue shall confess that Jesus Christ is truly Lord. So you see it's not mere chance that caused an angel one night long ago to say to a virgin maiden, "His name shall be called Jesus, because he shall save his people from their sins" (Matthew 1:21).[1]

It's those same words that are used to describe the name of Jesus by Gloria Gaither that can also be used to describe the body of the Lord Jesus Christ. Countless attempts have been made to de-legitimize our influence, kill our progress, and stamp out our identity, yet the gates of hell have not prevailed. We march forward, bringing the kingdom of heaven to more of the earth and accelerating the second coming of the Lord Jesus Christ by doing so.

I invite you to journey with me over the following chapters as we look at this glorious, triumphant church that, while full of flaws and imperfect people, is beautifully and wonderfully made as the only vehicle that will bring humankind to salvation. We're a mess, and we'll admit it.

We're flawed, and we know it. But we're still here, we're still triumphant, and we still have a destiny before us because it was said so long ago: The gates of hell shall not prevail against the church.

2

A Book-of-Acts Church

The message of our triumphant church was first born inside of me when the Lord challenged me to take a step of faith as a young pastor. God had basically taken me out of my comfort zone and said, "Now, it's time to go on your own and trust in me alone." I was too dependent on people and systems, and the Lord was about to teach me that he alone was my source, my counselor, my provider, and more than that, he was the Head of his body.

Through faith, I took the steps the Lord was calling me to take, and I launched out on my own and began pastoring a very small church in Virginia. Our congregation had begun with just a family of five, but it had grown to a few hundred people over the first two or three years. We had rapid growth. We had the signs of favor. By the time we were a four-year-old congregation, we were able to purchase an amazing property on our own—twenty-eight thousand square feet, a three hundred-seat sanctuary, and an eighteen-classroom school building that we later turned into a community center.

When I heard the property was available for purchase, I asked my assistant pastor to accompany me there so that we could pray. The night I went to pray over the building and ask the Lord for his will and favor, I heard the Lord speak. He asked me a question. He said, "Why do you ask for what is already yours?" My faith was challenged. Though we were a young congregation with very limited resources and no financial history to tell of, God said the building was ours.

From there, everything within the church moved quickly. Sacrificial giving and finances increased. We were successful in purchasing the property and began renovating according to the needs of our congregation. Then we accrued a staff and involved ourselves in the community. We knew that when the gospel is applied to every area of your life, every area of your life will change. We sought to be holistic in our teaching and preaching. We celebrated the greatest miracle of all: salvation, but we also wanted to see people heal and be whole, prosperous, joyful, and leading victorious lives.

We opened a community center that allowed us to engage our community through a variety of means: from teaching English classes and hosting citizenship seminars to offering crisis counseling and teaching music lessons. We empowered members of the church to launch out on their own and begin their own businesses.

Our congregation was primarily made up of first generation immigrants to the United States. It's said that one in four immigrants to the United States will become entrepreneurs. Knowing the likelihood that many of the individuals in our congregation would own their own business one day, we attempted to connect those aspiring entrepreneurs with established business owners who could serve as mentors and assist them in establishing their own businesses.

We made computers available to students within our congregation who didn't have a computer in their home. Our congregation managed to accomplish a lot in a short amount of time. It seemed miraculous to us. God was faithful. It was the best of times, but we were also doing a lot of things spontaneously. The honeymoon period for our church was quickly coming to an end as reality set in. People were joining the church, but they were also leaving. We weren't as prepared as we needed to be for the growth and responsibility that had come our way.

One week I came home frustrated and told my late wife, Jessica, "It's like we're pastoring a carwash."

"What does that mean?" Jessica asked.

I said, "They leave as fast as they come. It's like they come into the church, they repent, they're baptized, God changes their lives, and then they're off to another ministry. We clean them up and ship them out."

When frustrations like these happen, I think there's a natural tendency for many of us to feel indignant. We think, "You want to leave *our* church? Us? I thought our church was awesome!" (And what pastor doesn't?)

I couldn't understand why anybody would want to leave our church. Some people thought I was too young to be leading the church. Some said we were "too white for a Hispanic church," or we were "too Hispanic" for others.

I've learned that time is always our best friend. As I reflect on those days, I've gained perspective and come to understand and accept my share of the blame for some of the criticisms, but at the time, I was perplexed. I thought we had a good thing going and couldn't understand why we now seemed to be in a time of trouble.

I attended an old-fashioned church camp meeting during this period of struggle. The preacher who was speaking that night was a Pentecostal preacher for whom I had a lot of admiration. As he came to the close of his message he said, "I believe there are some pastors here who are going home to a struggling church. You're going home to a church that's divided, and it's struggling, and you've been saying, 'Oh, God! What is the answer for my church? What shall I do for my church?'" He went on to say in a thundering and booming baritone voice, "I've come to tell you that what you need to do is go home and pray, 'Oh God, give me a book-of-Acts church!'"

Everybody went wild, including myself. It was as if he was talking directly to me, so I prayed exactly that prayer. I was earnestly praying and crying out to him. I lifted my voice and said, "Oh God, give me a book-of-Acts church!" *And God answered!*

Sometimes we spend so much time talking during prayer that we forget prayer should be a conversation with God. We intentionally bring our petitions to him, but we also need to intentionally set aside time where we purposefully listen for the voice of God. If prayer is having a conversation with God, it means we have to both talk and listen. My mother taught me as a young child that part of prayer is listening for the voice of God because God is a gentleman who knocks at the door; the Bible doesn't say he kicks the door down. He kicked the tables over in a temple one time, but he knocks on the door of your heart, and he waits for you to answer the door. We talk to him, and we pray, "Speak to me about my marriage, speak to me about my money, speak to me about my ministry. Help me here, help me there. In the name of Jesus, amen."

God tries to give us a word, but he doesn't interrupt us. We know that in the beginning was the Word, and the Word was with God, and the Word was God. The Spanish translation of that verse replaces the word *word* with "verb." I enjoy that translation more. God speaks in "verbs" because we know that when he speaks, it's creative, life-changing, life-altering, and it *shall* come to pass. He's ready to release the word we need, yet we keep cutting him off with another demand, another request, or another petition. Sometimes we leave him out, and we don't listen.

There I was crying out, "Help this church, God. Give me a book-of-Acts church!" And that very night I heard God speak back to me.

He asked, "Have you read the book of Acts?"

I honestly felt taken aback by what I heard, and quite frankly, I didn't understand what he was saying to me. I thought, "Wait a second. I work for you. I come from a family line that for three generations has proudly served you and preached this gospel message. Of course, I've read the book of Acts!"

"But did you *really* read the book of Acts?"

Again, I thought, "What does that mean? Yes, I read it!"

I was dismayed, perplexed, and surprised that God would ask such a question of me—a third generation Pentecostal! I don't know anything but the book of Acts. If there's any book of the Bible that the charismatic Pentecostal movement knows, we know the book of Acts.

About Acts

Now, in case you aren't as familiar with the book of Acts, don't worry, because I will catch you up on it throughout the next few chapters. You'll read with me how God caused his church to become triumphant despite their mess, but first, we should understand the setting into which this incredible book is set.

Acts is so named because it records the acts of the apostles after Jesus ascended into heaven. Of course, this means all the content in the book of Acts came after Jesus' life, ministry, death, and resurrection. Jesus ministered for only three or four years on earth and chose twelve men to be his disciples. Imagine yourself among the disciples in those days. Many other men and women followed Jesus closely, but these twelve were his closest followers. They didn't get along, they frequently argued, and when the darkest moment came as Jesus went through his trials and was led away to be crucified, all but one of them abandoned him.

This is the group of men, along with about a hundred others, to whom Jesus entrusted the fate of the world. He told them about his kingdom, then left them on earth to build it. The book of Acts records the first steps the disciples took to build the church and the first years of what we now call church history.

As you imagine living in those days, how do you think this might turn out? What problems do you think they might encounter? Do you even see it working at all?

Maybe it seems impossible, and it was, but they served a God of the impossible, just as we do today. You are about to see not only the mistakes they made as humans, but also the impossible marvels God worked among them in the development of his triumphant church.

3

Rushing Ahead

In obedience to God's challenge to read through the books of Acts, I began to study the book of Acts—again, but I read it with new eyes so to speak. It was as if there was a veil over my eyes that was lifted. I read things I had never read before. At times, the more I read the more disappointed and depressed I felt. The early church dealt with so much drama; it was a mess. The church faced problems from its very inception. It was so rife with trial and tribulation that I read it and thought, "You know what? On second thought, we have a great church ... maybe I don't need a 'book-of-Acts' church after all."

Confusion and Desertion

Chapter one starts by reminding us of the resurrection of Jesus Christ, and how he revealed himself to the apostles many times over a forty-day period. During these times,

Jesus shared with them truths of God's kingdom and gave them instructions. He specifically commanded the apostles not to leave Jerusalem, but to wait there for the promise of the Father. That promise, or fulfillment of the promise, would make them "baptized and empowered and united with the Holy Spirit" (Acts 1:5 AMP).

All of this took place on the Mount of Olives just before Jesus ascended into the heavens. He told them, "But you will receive power and ability when the Holy Spirit comes upon you; and you will be My witnesses [to tell people about Me] both in Jerusalem and in all Judea, and Samaria, and even to the ends of the earth" (Acts 1:8 AMP). I imagine the apostles were looking up and waving goodbye as the Son of Man ascended into the clouds. The Bible says two angels appeared and saw them gazing up at the sky, and the angels said, "Go to work. Go wait." This had to blow the minds of the apostles, but one angel says, "The same Jesus that you saw leave is coming back, the same way in which he left."

Remember, the apostles were not theologians in any sense of the word. They were former fishermen, doctors, and members of society who were hardly considered epitomes of the faith. Their calls to ministry lacked all the grandeur and ceremony of ordination and consecration services that we see in the modern-day church. There was no holy convocation or ceremonial equivalent. These were simply people to whom Jesus had called out, "Follow me," and they followed him. They learned less by what Jesus taught as lessons one, two, and three, but more by simply being in his presence and experiencing what they saw and felt.

The command of Jesus was simply to wait on the

promise of the Father; that was it. It's my opinion that they didn't even have a solid understanding of what the promise of the Father was going to be. All they knew was Jesus charged them to go to Jerusalem and wait: "You shall become efficient, capable, and mighty, when the Holy Spirit has come upon you" (Acts 1:8 AMPC). Obediently, the disciples went to Jerusalem and into a second-floor room—the upper room—and they prayed.

They knew his promise was going to empower them. That was great, but nobody knew what the promise was or when it was coming. Was someone new going to walk through the door? They didn't know what they were waiting for, and they didn't know how to wait. They were confused. Depending on the source, up to five hundred people initially went with the apostles to Jerusalem, and of the hundreds of people who followed, only one hundred and twenty stayed until the fulfillment of the promise of the Father occurred. While there was promise and potential, the church was just beginning, and there was already impatience, confusion, and desertion with the plan of God.

Impatience

While waiting for the promise of the Father, a conversation about Judas ensues. We'll never know how this conversation started, but I imagine someone said, "So ... Judas! That was bad, huh? I can't believe he did that. Well, you know, Judas was always kind of sketchy. Did you see him messing with that bowl when we were having dinner with Jesus?"

Their conversation appears to have inspired Peter to utilize his newfound keys to the kingdom. He launched into a theological dissertation about how Judas was used to accomplish God's purpose and fulfill Scripture. Sometimes we preachers find ourselves on a tangent when we get excited about something, and Peter was no different. In fact, he seems to have become a little too motivated from his own explanation because his analysis led him to believe that they needed a twelfth apostle, and they needed one right then and there.

Here's what's interesting to me: They prayed before deciding on the next apostle. They prayed, "Oh, Lord Jesus, guide our decision. Help us name a leader." But then they took matters into their own hands by casting lots.

It's as if they asked themselves, "Well, how do you name leaders?"

"I don't know."

"Well, how did Jesus do it?"

"I don't know. He just pointed and said, 'Follow me.'"

"How should we do it?"

"Let's draw straws. Surely, that's a great way to do it. God will bless the drawing of the straws." Now, some would argue this is akin to an election. Others will say it's a game of chance. Regardless, they asked the Lord to show them who to pick and then picked someone for themselves.

"The shortest straw belongs to ... Matthias! Congratulations, Matthias, you're the twelfth apostle. Welcome to the club."

I'm sure Matthias was a good man and brother in the Lord, but you never read about him again. I'm not criticizing Matthias or saying anything unjust about him. I realize we don't know everything about the circumstances of the upper room. What's important to understand is that Matthias was not appointed by Jesus; he was chosen by man, and he was chosen before the promise of the Father was fulfilled. The apostles were taking action when they were supposed to be waiting. Matthias loved Jesus and walked with him, but Jesus had not appointed him.

Poor Leadership Appointment

One of the many lessons from chapter one is that just because someone follows and loves Jesus doesn't necessarily mean they're also called into leadership. There were one hundred and twenty people who loved Jesus, received the promise, and waited on its fulfillment. The disciples had over one hundred people to choose from. We know now as we look back that God already had a plan for the twelfth apostle; we know it's to be the apostle Paul. Of course, they neither knew nor understood this while they were in the upper room.

Herein we find a classic, perpetual problem: They prayed to the Lord, but they didn't wait on the Lord. The disciples were supposed to be waiting, yet they were acting. They took it upon themselves to name a twelfth apostle—just in case God didn't already have a plan, and they made a poor leadership appointment. It's frustrating to read, and most of us probably ask ourselves (and Peter), *Why would Peter take it upon himself to make a leadership decision prior to the fulfillment of the promise? Why, Peter?! Why would you do that when what's promised to you is going to make you able, efficient, and mighty?*

Timing Is Everything

Let's discuss how many churches and ministries struggle and hurt because of poor leadership appointments. At our church in Virginia, we were practically naming leaders for the sake of having leaders. We were approaching people saying, "Hey! We're starting a youth ministry next week. Could you be our youth pastor? Have you ever been a deacon? No? Well, do you want to be?"

Okay, so it wasn't that bad, but we were moving full steam ahead. It sounded like a good idea to us at the time, and it certainly felt good to grow, but we did things ahead of schedule and outside of God's timing because we were anxious to move and grow quickly.

Patience is not a virtue that many people possess—the apostles (and myself) included. Impatience often causes us to make decisions that we later realize we shouldn't have made. Chances are, we've all been like Peter at least one time or another (or many other times). Whether or not you've already learned this lesson in your walk with God, timing is everything. You can try to push God's timing ahead, but you'll ultimately find that it's best to operate on God's clock.

Acts 1 tells me that just because you have a promise doesn't mean you have permission to get ahead of God's timing. Just because there's potential, and just because you don't understand, that doesn't mean you should attempt to define what the promise is, jump ahead, or even "help" God. How many times has God given us a promise that we don't understand? Arguably, almost every time. Sometimes it appears as though he gives us the key to a door without telling us what lies behind it, or even which door the key unlocks. Sometimes he trusts us to try every door.

God's Clock

I remember one night in Chicago when I really needed an answer from God. I was facing a major decision, and I had my own opinion about what I thought I wanted and needed. I went to the sanctuary of the church in which I was raised to pray. I was able to get into the building since I had the keys (perks of being a pastor's kid), and I locked myself in the sanctuary.

I had a good, long prayer meeting with the Lord. I began to name and claim and decree and declare. I began to speak things as though they were, and I claimed all the Bible verses that were a benefit to me. I said that every good and perfect gift comes from the Father who's above. I said, "It is written that you will give me the desires of my heart." I said, "It is written where two or three come into agreement. Jesus, you and I are coming into agreement. We're coming into agreement, and this is what I desire. I speak it. I confess it. I declare it. Let it be so. Let it be done. I'll give you the praise and the glory. Father, give me the desires of my heart, and let your will be done, in Jesus' name."

When I finished the prayer, I heard the Lord speak back to me. He said, "Well, which one do you want?"

I said, "What do you mean?"

He said, "Well you asked me for two things. You asked me for the desires of your heart, and then you said thy will be done. Which one do you want? Do you want your desires, or do you want my will?"

It's a personal story, so I won't share the details, but there was indeed a difference between my desires and the will of God in that situation. I thought I could help accelerate God's clock in heaven. I want to thank the Lord. It's been years since that happened, but I want to thank him for asking that question and that his will was done and not the desires of my heart. If he'd given me the desires of my heart, then I don't know if I'd be preaching today.

Sometimes we run ahead with our own plans, and it leads us down roads God never intended for us to travel. It can lead to pain, suffering, and loss, or it can simply lead to delays, wasted time, and frustration. Yes, God can and will always redeem our mistakes if we confess them to him and begin following him again, but how much simpler would it be if we just waited on him from the start?

This is one lesson I needed to learn, and it was a lesson the apostles needed to learn too. We see them running ahead of the Lord even while they are waiting for his promise. This isn't a good start to the "Acts of the Apostles." Would it get better in chapter two?

4

Conflict of Every Kind

Confusion, desertion, impatience, and poor leadership appointments plague chapter one. That was not a good start, but then I read chapter two, which turned out to be no more encouraging.

When the promise of the Father finally came, we read of a sound from heaven that was "as of a rushing, mighty wind" that filled the house (Acts 2:2 KJV). The apostles and the followers in the upper room became filled with the baptism of the Holy Spirit and began speaking in tongues and languages they had never known. The promise of the Father had finally descended onto the apostles who had tarried in the upper room. The triumphant, victorious church was being born on the inside!

The people of the city heard the roaring sound, and a crowd gathered outside the upper room. The people in the crowd were amazed: "'How can this be?' they exclaimed. 'These people are all from Galilee, and yet we hear them speaking in our own native languages'" (Acts 1:7-8 NLT). Some of the people of the city made a mockery of them and accused them of being crazy or drunk, which was especially insulting since the Bible says the fulfillment took place at nine in the morning.

The people in the crowd couldn't see what the faithful saw. They couldn't feel what the faithful felt. They didn't understand what was taking place, but what was taking place in that room was the reception of the fulfillment of the promise for which they had waited upon God. They heard, they waited, and they received. The church was newly empowered, and immediately and simultaneously it was mocked and discredited.

Can you imagine waiting for this promise of power, and when it occurs it's instantly met with mockery? Peter and the apostles knew very well that Jesus said the gates of hell would not prevail against the church. They were aware that they were to be witness in Jerusalem, Judea, and beyond. But how do you spread what is supposed to be a powerful message if it's ridiculed from the onset?

Poverty and Persecution

In chapter three, Peter and John were on their way to church when they found a lame man sitting at the door. He was seeking alms, yet every day the faithful would pass him by, and he wasn't getting healed.

I'm a visual person, and I can envision this moment like a scene in a movie. I see this man being carried to church and the faithful followers walking around and stepping over him. I see a church that is so preoccupied with getting their blessing, their miracle, and their answered prayer that they never even stop to consider him. This man begged Peter and John for money, and Peter said, "Silver or gold I do not have, but what I do have I give you. In the name of Jesus Christ of Nazareth, walk" (Acts 3:6 NIV). The man was healed! I say this mostly in jest, but it's humorous to me to read the first sentence of Acts 3:5 "Silver and gold I do not have." The ministry was already broke. Even without gold and silver, however, they possessed a power from on high.

Regardless of how many times the lame man had been overlooked and passed by, when the apostles of the Lord Jesus Christ took notice of him and commanded him to walk in Jesus' name, he did exactly that. He walked, he leapt, and he praised God.

Dumbfounded over the miracle they had just witnessed, a crowd gathered. Peter used that opportunity to preach to them the power of God, and the souls of five thousand people were saved that day. What was Peter's and John's honorarium for their message and ministry, their blessing for healing and preaching? They were arrested and thrown into prison. In Acts 3, I read of a bankrupt church that was persecuted and punished for performing miracles, and one that arguably lacked a bit of empathy.

Rather than celebrate the miraculous healing that took place in chapter three, Peter and John are questioned in chapter four by authorities who grill them: "Who gave you the power to heal that man?" It's interesting because those who confronted Peter and John don't deny the miraculous work of the apostles, but the miracle still does not convince them to believe.

Not knowing what to do with Peter and John, the authorities decided that to "stop this thing from spreading any further among the people, we must warn them to speak no longer to anyone in this name" (Acts 4:17 NIV). Even though the naysayers were unable to deny what was taking place, Peter and John were still persecuted and forbidden from teaching or preaching anything more in the name of the Lord Jesus Christ.

Deceit

At the end of chapter four, all the believers in the church sold everything they had and laid their proceeds at the feet of the apostles. This felt like a turn for the better but quickly proved otherwise. At the very the beginning of chapter five, Ananias and his wife, Sapphira, sold their farm and tried to offer only a portion of their proceeds to the apostles instead of their entire profit. There would have been nothing wrong with that; they were free to do with their money and their property as they chose.

The problem was that Ananias and Sapphira lied. They told the church they were giving all of their proceeds from the sale of their property, but the reality was they only gave part of it and kept the rest. They lied to the man of God, and they lied to the Holy Spirit. The church was barely established, and there was already lying and deceit. An abundance of miracles also took place in chapter five, and despite their good work, the apostles continued to be arrested, beaten, and imprisoned for preaching and healing.

The church in Acts 6 was still thriving financially. The apostles didn't need to preach about money. There were no stewardship campaigns; they didn't have to beg. The believers were laying all their money at the feet of the apostles. The church was so blessed that they even had the necessary finances to take care of the widows and orphans. I read, "And in those days, when the number of the disciples was multiplied" (Acts 6:1 KJV). I said, "Hey, Jesus! Do that for me!" I started thanking God that he isn't a God of addition; he's a God of multiplication. I became excited! But then I saw the comma. The verse goes on to say, "there arose a murmuring."

Division, Murder, and Corruption

I had thought growing and revival were the solutions to church problems. It turned out that, according to the Bible, the more you grow, and the more you have, the more issues arise. And that's not simply because of the attack from the enemy, but sometimes even blessings can cause problems. The church was so blessed that they actually started complaining about the blessing. The widows rose up and said, "How come she has more than me? Why did she eat first? How come I never get to go first?" Now we find division and jealousy within the church of the Lord Jesus Christ of the first century.

In Acts 7, a mighty, fiery evangelist by the name of Stephen was stoned to death for preaching the gospel.

Members of the church now risked being murdered. Then Simon the Sorcerer, renowned for his magic, was baptized after hearing an apostle preach the name of Jesus. Simon later witnessed Peter and John impart the power of God by baptizing Samaritan believers in the Holy Spirit simply by laying their hands on them. Amazed by such power, Simon attempted to offer money to Peter and John with the hopes of gaining such power for himself. Peter and John severely rebuked Simon; nevertheless, corruption was born into the church that day.

Legalism and Prejudice

Saul of Tarsus, who took part in the stoning of Stephen and had persecuted the church, encountered Jesus on the road to Damascus in chapter nine. Saul repented and converted to Christianity, and his conversion was so strong that not only did he have an identity change, but he also had a name change. Unsurprisingly, the Jewish people and the Christians who had already received Jesus struggled to accept Saul. It was hard for them to believe that the same blood that had been shed for them could also be shed for the violent Saul of Tarsus. Some of the Jews even tried to kill him, the man who's later known as the apostle Paul and the true twelfth apostle. In chapter nine, we read of a church that was making decisions about who could and could not be saved. We find the birth of legalism and judgmentalism within the church of the Lord Jesus Christ in chapter nine.

Then I read Acts 10, which I believe is very relevant to our present-day. God decided to reveal the fullness of his truth to Cornelius, a devout man who feared the Lord, who was hungry for the things of the Lord, and who was crying out to God. God called on Peter to go to him, but Peter essentially said, "No, no, no. We don't preach to those people. We don't preach to that tribe. We don't go to those people. They're dirty; they're not like us. We don't go to those houses because this message is only for a select few." Even in the first century, we find prejudice and racism in the church of the Lord Jesus Christ.

The Problems Never Stop

In chapter eleven, Peter had to answer for his decision to preach to the people of Cornelius' house. That's akin to being summoned before a denominational or district board. Later in the book of Acts, the apostle Paul must have been giving some mighty good preaching because a young man falls asleep and out of the window. It would appear that the struggle to keep young people engaged has been going on since the first century. As my friend Bishop Angel Marcial once told me, the only way the church is going to reach young people is for the church to get down on their level. As if the problems from the first ten chapters weren't enough, Peter was now having to justify his decisions, and Paul was boring people to sleep.

The book of Acts continues, and we start to follow Paul through his missionary journeys, and his problems are famous. Paul's first attempt as a missionary to reach people with the gospel was to go to the synagogue and preach to the Jews. It started off well enough until the Jewish leaders became jealous and stirred up trouble against him. This exact same pattern repeated itself for decades, forcing Paul to flee from city to city because the Jews chased him everywhere he went, trying to kill him.

It was hardly better when Paul went to preach to gentiles. He was beaten, whipped, falsely imprisoned, accused of starting riots and inciting plots against the emperor, stoned, left for dead, shipwrecked, and more. Is that what I was asking for when I cried out for a book-of-Acts church?

The gospel didn't even come out clearly in all the places Paul preached. Athens simply said, "Well, that's interesting. We'd like to hear more," but nothing happened there. It was just tickling curious ears without touching any hearts. In more than one city, the people saw Paul perform miracles, and they began to worship him as a god. Paul and his companions worked hard to keep these "converts" from blaspheming against God and instead redirect them toward Jesus.

Paul's problems weren't limited to his audience, either. His first partner, Barnabas, sharply disagreed with Paul over another believer, and they parted ways. Paul chose another ministry partner, Silas, to join him on his missionary journeys. Division and strife broke apart one of the most fruitful ministry pairs in history.

We could keep going through every single chapter in Acts and we would find problem after problem after problem. Going all the way back to the first days of the church, we find issues of confusion, poor leadership, impatience, persecution, greed, division, deceit, murder, discrimination, legalism, strife, and prejudice. The church was rife with every kind of conflict.

Any one of those issues is discouraging, let alone all of them. I grew so discouraged I nearly stopped reading. This was the first-century church that every church elder longs to have? This is the church we look to as the epitome of revival and success, as the gold standard of what a church should be? I felt the Holy Spirit ask me, "Are you sure you want a church like the book of Acts?"

5

"Read It Again"

I was still pastoring this small, struggling church as I was studying Acts again. Our church was experiencing division and fighting gossip. I had read the first ten chapters and was feeling disheartened when the Lord said, "Read it again."

I read it a second time, and I no longer saw all the issues. It was as if God had lifted the veil from my eyes that had been blinding me from seeing the upper room, the Holy Ghost being poured out, the signs, the miracles, the wonders, the expansion, the revival, and the multiplication. Before, all I had seen were problems. This time, all I saw was victory.

The church was absolutely experiencing issues in Acts 1, but you also find God giving a promise to the church, a covenant. He'd declared to them, "You shall receive power after the Holy Ghost has come upon you. You will be witnesses. You will do this. You will do that." Even though there were leadership issues and trouble while they waited on the Lord, all those things were ultimately side issues compared to the Word of the Lord: This church would have power after the Holy Ghost has come upon it. He commissioned the church, and he was preparing them for success. He'd given them the Word, and we know the Word of God cannot return void.

Expectancy

The apostles were flawed, but they waited faithfully for the promise of God when others abandoned the upper room. I believe expectancy draws God into situations, and the apostles' expectancy of the Father's promise was like a magnetic force. Expectancy is not fingers-crossed hoping; expectancy is like a kid on Christmas—one eye closed, one eye opened, hands extended, waiting for a gift to be placed into them.

I first learned the power of expectancy, or the level of faith called expectancy, some years ago at a healing crusade in Chicago. I sat and watched multiple people who were wheelchair-bound stand up, walk away, and be healed during the worship. While this was going on, I left the healing crusade because I felt the urging of the Holy Spirit to go out of the stadium and into the lobby. Security personnel were blocking the door because the venue had reached its maximum capacity. People were yanking on the door crying, "Let me in! Let me in!" These ladies were outside shouting for their entry.

One lady screamed at security, "Let me in! Don't you

get it? If I just get in the building, I'm going to get a miracle." I'll never know who that lady was, but she changed my life. She blew me away. She was so convinced that if she could just get in the door, a miracle would happen. I'd never encountered faith like that. I encountered hope—hope for healing, hope for things to work out. She was confident and ready to have a throw-down fistfight with security.

God said to me, "See her? She expects. You've been hoping, but do you believe I could do it?"

I said, "Well, you're God."

He said, "I know who I am. I'm asking if you believe that I can do this?"

I learned expectancy, and that's what took place in Acts 2. They were expecting, they were longing, they were hungry, they were thirsty for the promise of the Father, and then it came. They didn't know what to expect. There was already confusion and problems with leadership, but here came the promise of the Father.

Fulfillment

A significant event had captured the attention of the entire city on the day of the fulfillment. As the city gazed upon the upper room, everybody in Jerusalem became aware that something had taken place. They heard the apostles speaking in the languages of the people who were in that city. Suddenly, people were exposed to the gospel of the Lord Jesus Christ, and they understood the message.

That's incredibly prophetic to me. Out of chaos came clarity. Out of tongues came a message. Thousands of people were converted that day, and thousands were baptized because the apostles waited faithfully, and God fulfilled his promise. When God moves and fulfills his promise, prophecy is fulfilled.

When the Holy Spirit comes upon you, it's not just to make you speak in other tongues like it was for the apostles. It's not some kind of second blessing. The power of God comes upon you not for your own glory, but for the glory of the name of Christ and for the work of the kingdom of God on earth—to see the kingdom expand.

I heard this phrase from a ministry once: "The dunamis power of God." The dunamis power of God is supernatural power. When God's dunamis power comes upon you through the Holy Spirit, you become able to do things that otherwise you could not do. The apostles and disciples in the upper room demonstrated this by speaking in tongues, but Peter also demonstrated it by preaching a sermon with a power that led three thousand souls to repent, become saved, and get baptized.

This was all humanly impossible. None of those men or women had been able to do any of those things in the moments before the Holy Spirit came upon them. It is the same way with you and me. We can do many things in our own strength and effort, but God offers us something much better. He offers us his dunamis power through his Holy Spirit. Through this power and through the Holy Spirit, you become able to do things that are humanly impossible. One of the things this means is that you become efficient.

Efficiency

To me, efficiency means you are able to make something happen. Every good church, every revival church, every church ordered by the Holy Spirit, will be able to speak to heaven and man. The Holy Spirit will make you able to speak the tongues and the language of the earth. You'll be able to receive a blessing of heaven, contextualize it, and minister it to the community around you. That's precisely what's taking place in the book of Acts: God made the apostles efficient; the people of the city were then able to hear, and thus a prophetic occurrence took place.

God has spoken things to me and has told me to do things that sounded crazy. Not everyone understands what God promises us. They don't understand what God's doing in my life or in your life, but don't let go of the promise of the Father. Don't be guilty of walking out before the promise of the Father is fulfilled. Don't walk ahead of his time. God helped me to understand that the Father goes before us and opens the door that no human can shut.

His Word Shall Come to Pass

The fulfillment of the promise came to the disciples, and it didn't matter that the apostles were mocked and discredited as drunken lunatics. It was hardly the first time that God's followers were ridiculed, undermined, or persecuted. Abraham heard God, but Sarah laughed at the Word. Noah heard God, and the community made fun of him. Joseph heard and dreamt of God, and his brothers conspired against him. Daniel heard and prayed to God, and his peers tried to kill him. Jonah heard God, and he ended up in the belly of a whale.

Following God almost always requires you to be misunderstood. It's almost a certainty that you will be misunderstood by your family, friends, community, and everyone else when you hear and obey his voice because no one has heard what you've heard. That's okay; let them mock you. They haven't had the experience with God that you've had, but you've heard the promise of the Father. You're waiting for the fulfillment, and when God gives you a promise, you don't let go of it until it comes to pass.

Grace, mercy, and goodness follow us all the days of our lives. Goodness and mercy are picking up the gifts, the anointing, the ministry, the money, and the talents that you lost or misplaced along the way. The Bible says that his angels encamp around you. You want to know why you're stepping into your promised land and why you're making it into the next season of your life? Because God has gone before you; goodness and mercy are following you. The angels of the Lord are encamped around you, protecting your destiny and protecting your promise.

The Bible says the earth shall pass away, but His Word shall not return void. You might have to wait ten days in an upper room, you might have to walk around a mountain for forty years, you might have to sleep in the belly of a whale for three days and three nights, but if he spoke it, it shall come to pass. You will enter the Promised Land.

You will receive the promise of the Father, and you will be endued by the power of the Holy Spirit. You will become able and efficient, and you will do the work of God on earth, but you must wait it out. You must wait it out through mockery, scorn, criticism, and gossip. I declare to you in the name of Jesus that just like the promise of the Father came in Acts 2, your promise is coming to pass.

6

God Fulfilling His Word

The first time I reread Acts, all I could see was the mess that filled the church page after page and chapter after chapter. The second time I reread Acts, I had the opposite experience: I saw God's faithfulness. I saw a church that overcame. I saw revival breaking out, growing, and multiplying. I saw a city being changed by the power of God fulfilling his Word.

As I continued reading, I saw that even in the face of mockery, Peter had the courage to preach a sermon to the crowd after they left the upper room in Acts 2. He was mocked but continued to lift up the name of Jesus, and he helped save thousands of people that day. I wonder what it was like to be there and hear the message of the gospel for the first time. This was the same Peter who had denied Jesus a few months earlier, and now he was declaring the name of the Lord strongly and mightily to these people in Jerusalem.

Unity in Leadership, Abundant Miracles, and a Generous Church

The Bible says that when Peter stood, the other eleven stood with him. That's symbolic to me. They knew Peter and all of his mess. They knew he had cut off a servant's ear, denied Jesus, and failed when he tried to walk on water. Those things didn't matter to them. Peter preached the message, and no one said, "No, Peter, that's not how I said it in my book. I'm writing it differently." They stood in agreement. When God appoints you to anointed leadership, those around you sense it. The assignment of the church is to stand with its leadership, just like the eleven other apostles stood with Peter. This unity brings the favor of God on your life.

I was so dismayed by the church's lack of compassion toward the lame man in chapter three that I failed to appreciate all the incredible miracles that were taking place in that very same chapter. So many miracles were happening that people were absolutely clamoring for them. After John and Peter healed the lame man, he left the church dancing, leaping, and praising the Lord. Sure, the church should have shown more compassion, but I had completely missed the wondrousness of the abundant healings happening throughout Jerusalem.

I also failed to see that salvations were truly more rampant than the struggles during that time. If compassion was on short order in the church, perhaps it was because the church was growing so quickly that it made discipleship quite hard. This is a work of God!

Acts 4 begins with Peter and John's arrest for preaching the name of Jesus, yes, but their arrest is a testament to the amazement of the religious leaders who suddenly recognized Peter and John had truly been with Jesus because of the fire in their words. When they released Peter and John, these two leaders went back to the church where they worshiped and prayed so fervently the ground shook, and they were filled with the Holy Spirit even more.

Acts 4 ends with the body of believers selling their possessions, giving away everything they had, and laying it at the feet of the apostles. Essentially, they had said, "Whatever we have is nothing compared to what God has given us, so we'll lay it back at the feet of the Lord, so that the gospel of Jesus Christ can be propagated throughout the land and nation." They gave freely to the work of the ministry. All the work that was being done was made possible by a generous church.

Acts 5 records that the miracle-working power of God was so incredibly strong amongst the apostles that the sick simply laid out in the streets, so that as the shadow of Peter passed over them, they were healed! It tells us that extraordinary miracles were worked through the hands of the other apostles as well. They were so filled with the boldness and power of God that even when they were persecuted, they rejoiced that they had lived worthy of Jesus enough to have earned attention from the opposition. Persecution would not keep them down.

In Acts 6, amongst the grumbling and complaining, and while arguing about who had more food, the number of disciples was multiplied. God was adding daily to his church. The complaining wasn't stopping growth. In fact, it only served as an opportunity for the apostles to raise up more leaders whom they could trust. The complaints strengthened the church because they implemented much-needed structure and allowed the apostles to focus solely on praying and preaching.

Acts 7 tells that Stephen is murdered, but not before lives are birthed into the kingdom. This martyr saw the face and heard the voice of the God who he had preached about and for whom was willing to die. Then in Acts 8, the believers were scattered, and even though they were displaced from their homes, they filled every city and every area they found themselves in with the glorious gospel of Jesus Christ. They preached wherever they went. They were making Jesus famous. Many believed, and many were baptized and filled with the Holy Spirit. The persecution only further fulfilled Jesus' words that the church would be his witnesses to Judea, Samaria, and the ends of the earth.

Acts 9 reminds me of a song we used to sing in old Pentecostal services based on Zechariah 14:7: "There shall be light in the evening time." While the church dealt with persecution and the possibility of death for following Jesus, there was light in the darkness. In this particular instance, it was the darkness of Saul who saw the light of Jesus. Saul, the church's greatest human enemy, not only converted to following Jesus, but he also followed Jesus every bit as zealously as he had when he persecuted the church. He preached and argued with the Jews in Damascus, and when they chased him out, he preached and argued in Jerusalem.

After he left Jerusalem, the church experienced more growth than ever before, and it says they had peace.

In Acts 10, God showed that this gospel was for everyone who believed. Despite the Jewish laws that forbid Peter from visiting the home of a Gentile, Peter was led by the Holy Spirit to visit the home of Cornelius, a Roman military captain, and three of Cornelius' men (two servants and a soldier) to deliver a message. Peter's message was that everyone who believes in Jesus receives complete forgiveness. The Holy Spirit cascaded over everyone in the room with Peter, and he proceeded to baptize each and every one of them. This laid the foundation for the truth the apostle Paul would later write about: In the body of Christ, there is no longer Jew or Gentile, male or female (Galatians 3:27–28).

Throughout the book of Acts, from chapters 11 to 28, Paul performed even more miracles. When he was stoned and left for dead, he sprang back to life and reentered the city. When he was jailed with Silas, they worshiped, and God both set them free and gave them the power to baptize the souls of their jailer and his family. When Paul was shipwrecked, God delivered him each time, and at least one of those times God promised to give him the lives of everyone on the ship as well. In at least one city, the miraculous was so powerful in Paul's life that people would simply touch cloth to his skin and then give it to the sick and demonized, and they would be made whole.

It didn't matter how many trials he faced, how many cities he was chased out of, or how many times he was persecuted; he was triumphant and so was the church. At one point, the pagans even declared, "Those who have turned the world upside down have now come here!" That was the reputation of those early believers: They so moved in the boldness and power of God that they had turned the entire world upside down!

In every chapter of Acts, there was healing; there were miracles, signs, and wonders; there was expansion, deliverance, and salvation. Though they were persecuted, threatened, impoverished, misunderstood, and despite everything that was wrong with the first-century church, they were the church triumphant. What was their motivation? What drove the first-century church and all its progress? Jesus had told them, "I'm coming back again."

The body was working fiercely and passionately, so that all would know that there's one Lord, one faith, and one baptism. They were working passionately so that even those who had crucified Jesus would know that the same God they mocked, ridiculed, and crucified had died on the cross of Cavalry for them. They were trying to usher in the second coming of the Lord Jesus Christ.

Governments and officials could chain the hands and feet of the first-century church, but their voices would not remain silent. The apostles were falsely accused, tortured, and murdered, yet the sick people were still healed. How could that happen? It's because the church was not built on a philosophy. It was not built by mere mortals. It was built upon the words of Lord Jesus Christ.

7

Built upon the Word

Something that stands out to me—from Genesis to Revelation—is that God doesn't seem to be very interested in making a flashy or big entrance. He has the endings to stories down pat, and I mean this very respectfully, but it's the beginnings of the stories that seem underwhelming.

God forms Adam from dirt and Eve from a rib. He picks a pagan named Abram and makes him the father of our faith. He finds Moses hiding in a desert, and no one else is around to witness the burning bush. David is anointed king, and no one but his family is there to witness it (and his family is really only there because they're hoping that one of themselves is chosen for the anointing). God speaks to Daniel, but he mainly speaks to him when he's sleeping or praying privately.

Jesus, the Son of God, was born in a manger amongst animals. At Christmas, we try to liven up the scene and place the wise men near the manger, laying down the gold, frankincense, and myrrh at the feet of baby Jesus. We depict and clean up the event real nicely, but the truth is that at best, the wise men showed up maybe forty days after the birth of Jesus. They were late to the birthday party. Since Herod already wanted to kill all the boys under the age of two by that time, it's even plausible that Jesus could have been as old as one or even two years old by the time the wise men arrived.

The birth of the church falls in line with this same, underwhelming pattern. Its birth was no more glorious than Jesus' humble birth. Jesus was born in a stable, but at least shepherds worshiped, wise men visited, a star shone, and an angel sang. There was some kind of celebration for Jesus, but there was no such celebration for the birth of the church. It was arguably not off to the best of starts.

All of this is to say that God places a higher priority on enduring, winning, and finishing this race of life. It's not so much about how we begin, but rather how we finish the race. And no one wins a race or battle in a more dramatic fashion than God—seas part, walls fall, the earth shakes, and temple veils are torn. His grand finale for all earthly matters will be instant eternal redemption for humankind.

Revival in the Andes

My parents bought me a Bible when I was sixteen years old. My name was stamped on it in gold lettering, and it was the first Bible I ever took notes in. It was a preacher's Bible, and I proudly walked into services with it. When I was about eighteen years old, I started in ministry and took one of my first missions trips to Peru shortly thereafter. I was nineteen or twenty years old, and we were having a revival up in the Andes mountains. I went into that revival with my preacher's Bible, ready to let her rip in the name of Jesus.

The demonic manifested and showed itself in a young woman during that service. Forgive me if this sounds a little awkward, but this young woman was banging her head against the concrete floor. She was throwing her arms and legs, and the other preachers had her pinned down. There were probably four or five preachers on either side of her with their knees on top of her legs. Again, I'd been raised in the church all my life, but whenever those things took place, I left that stuff to the elders. I wanted to live in the feasting and the rejoicing, not so much in the fasting, praying, and sacrificing. I was young, and that's just who I was.

As this young woman was manifesting a demonic spirit, the missionary—who was probably three times older than me and had done so much more for the gospel and the cause of Christ than I have ever done in my life—looked at me and said, "Brother Suárez, come on over. We need you to pray."

I said, "Oh, but she's got a demon ..." I pulled out my preacher's Bible anyway and walked toward them with it extended at arm's length.

"And what is your name!" someone shouted, while everyone else was shouting something different.

The missionary said, "Stop. We're going to let Brother Suárez handle it."

I said, "Oh no, you're too kind. After you, sir. You take care of this situation."

I didn't know what to do, but I believed there was

power in the Word of God. All I knew to do was open my Bible and start reading. I started reading verses about the blood and the name of Jesus and forgiveness. As I was reading among the indigenous people of the Andes, that young lady sat up, looked at me, and suddenly yelled in English, "Don't read that!"

At that point, I was ready to come home to the United States. I was done. I said, "Lord, thank you for this opportunity. I'm going to sell cars, or suits, or do something. Anything else now." But I'm also a little stubborn. So, I did what any rational person would do: I kept reading the Word.

She kept screaming, "Don't read it! Don't read it!"

I thought I was safe because she was small and pinned down. The missionary was there, and I guess I thought he was some kind of Holy Ghost to shield her from me. She grabbed the Bible out of my hand, ripped the leather cover off, and started trying to rip the pages out. She managed to rip the leather, but she couldn't rip the paper. Eventually, she threw it back at me, and I heard the Lord speak.

He said, "Tony, the enemy will always be able to attack what's on the outside, but there's something he cannot destroy. There's something he can't come against. He cannot come against my Word. He cannot come against my promises. He cannot come against my covenant and the words that I have established over your life."

Every Word Accomplished

I've kept that Bible as a testimony because there have been many attacks and afflictions that have come my way, but the enemy has not been able to rip my life apart because it is built and predicated upon the Word of God. A lot of things have gone wrong in the church of the Lord Jesus Christ over the last two thousand years, but the reason we're still standing, and the reason we're still triumphant, and the reason we're still victorious is that we're built upon the foundation of the Word of God, and it is written that the gates of hell cannot and will not prevail against the church. We are built upon the teachings and the doctrines of the apostles and the prophets.

8

Hear His Voice

In 1952, a missionary named Joseph Knapp gave my grandfather a Bible in the country of Colombia. My grandfather took his newfound gift home to his family of thirteen children and his wife, and they began to read the Word daily. During this time, missionary Knapp was sent to a different part of the country, leaving my grandfather and that area without anyone to interpret and preach the Scriptures to them. As my family began reading the book of Acts, they wanted this "promise of the Father," but just like the believers of the first-century church that initially waited on the promise, no one knew what exactly they were waiting for.

My grandfather's solution was that they would not only read but also do what the people they were reading about did. Acts 2 said they gathered in one accord, so my grandfather, his family, and others from his area did the same. Acts 2 said they were in the upper room, so my grandfather took our family to a hill to pray and fast.

It was during that time that my uncle Rafael, who was eight years old at the time, testified to having been visited by an angel who told him where they would find "His Servant." After sharing with my grandfather what had happened to him, they embarked on a journey and, to their astonishment, found missionary William Thompson from England—just as the angel had spoken to Rafael. All of this occurred from simply doing what the early church did, and they had a supernatural experience like the early church did as well.

Unknowingly, my grandfather led his family to do exactly what we must do if we are to become a book-of-Acts church: We must know and listen to the voice of God. If we are going to be a book-of-Acts church that lives through setbacks, issues, and battles and still expand the kingdom of heaven on earth, and if we are to perform signs, miracles, wonders, and make disciples, we must learn what it is the apostles knew to obtain such victory. Most importantly, they knew the voice of God, and they followed it boldly.

The genesis of my journey through the book of Acts was hearing God challenge me to read through it. Can you say you've heard the voice of God? How can we do the work of God when we do not recognize or have never heard His voice? Learning to know his voice and discern what the Lord is saying could very well be the proverbial "most important lesson" in our walk with the Lord. By knowing his voice, I'll know his instruction and direction for my life.

We must be able to discern his voice and understand the different ways in which he might speak to us. Some hear an audible voice, like the Prophet Samuel heard in the temple, and others hear a smaller voice as did the Prophet

Elijah when he hid in the cave. Others have never heard an audible voice or even a smaller voice, but they recognize when God impresses something upon their hearts. Some of the most common ways to hear from the Lord are through reading His Word and listening to His Word as it's preached and taught. He desires to communicate with you. He has the answers to your every prayer.

The church in the book of Acts was a prayerful church, and by that I don't mean they simply brought petitions to the Lord. They prayed for direction from heaven as to what God wanted done on earth. They engaged in conversation with the Father, expecting and seeking his answer.

Talking vs. Listening

We often pray and ask the Lord for direction or an answer, but we don't give Him the opportunity to speak and answer us. As a child, I remember my mother leading our home church through something called a "prayer journey." Each room in the church represented different points of prayer on our journeys. One of the rooms was called the meditation room. In this room, there was no talking allowed, no music was played, and no one ministered. A person was to simply spend time in there just to listen.

Perhaps this concept seems strange, but think for a moment: What profit is to be gained by talking or making inquiries and petitions to someone without letting them respond? Prayer is a conversation with God. God spoke to his prophets and his disciples, and he wants to speak to us. It's our duty to learn to recognize his voice.

As a young teenager, I saw an evangelist named Morton Bustard minister and be used by God in a manner I had never seen before. He walked the aisles of the sanctuary of a church in central Illinois, led of the Spirit of God. He would stop in front of an individual, and without ever having met them, know their name and their affliction. I had never seen anything like it, and from that point on I was hooked.

I wondered, *How did he know? What did he hear? What did he see?* While the rest of us heard the sounds of people praising God, how could he hear beyond the noise and minister with perfect accuracy to an individual and their need? It was a throwback to things I had only read in the Bible, where God talked to his people. I wanted to experience it. I wanted to know how to discern God's voice. I began to spend a lot of time in prayer, asking the Lord to make me sensitive to his voice. I wanted to know when he was talking.

If You Ask, You Will Receive!

The result of those prayers was a "hearing test" from the Lord. What I learned from my hearing test was that he had always been speaking to me, but I didn't know how to recognize or discern his voice. During these prayer meetings, or hearing tests, I began to recognize his voice. At first, it had nothing to do with ministry. I experienced impressions on my heart and felt direction to make certain decisions.

At times I'd hear odd things that didn't make sense to me, yet I couldn't go on with my day without doing or accomplishing what I felt I had heard to do. Upon doing those things, the conviction or weight would lift. These hearing tests happened daily and then began to impact me as a minister.

One instance that I remember vividly was during one of my first trips to preach in California, where I was to minister to a small church in the southern part of the state. I was in my hotel room getting ready for the service and waiting for the driver to pick me up. I was ready to leave my room when something inside me said, "Look under the bed."

I thought, *How strange*, but decided to do it anyhow. Just as I had suspected, nothing was under the bed. I stood back up and was about to leave the room when yet again, something told me, "Look under the bed." Just as the first time, nothing was under the bed. I will admit that I started to wonder whether I was going crazy. I was hearing voices! I decided that this voice I was hearing was nothing, and I would walk out of my room regardless of what I felt or thought I was being told otherwise.

As I walked out the door something told me, "Go back and turn off the light." I opened the door, turned off the light, and shut the door. For the fourth time, this voice spoke to me and now said, "Open the door and turn on the light."

I couldn't stand it anymore. I said out loud, "Lord, what has happened to me? Am I going crazy? What is this?"

I can tell you with confidence that God answered me and said, "I was testing you! If you could not hear my voice when I sent you to look under the bed, and if you could not recognize my voice when I said to turn the lights off and then back on, how would you be able to hear me when

I speak to you tonight about that person who has cancer? If you cannot recognize my voice in something as simple as turning off the lights, you would not have been able to hear and recognize my voice when I speak to you about the needs of my people!"

My encounter with God in California was what I had been praying for, and the way I go about ministry was forever changed. He was teaching me to hear beyond the noise. I still pay attention to the small things because you never know what God will use to speak to you. The Bible teaches us that he gave direction to one prophet through a bush and to another by the mouth of a donkey. God can and will use anything to get our attention.

Depend on God's Word Always

You will never receive a "new revelation" that will change the truth contained in the sacred pages of the Word of God. God will never speak something to you that is contrary to what the Bible already says. His promises are "yes and amen." As you pursue God's heart and his truth, you will grow and learn to recognize his voice.

As I learned in my own life, hearing God's voice is important for everyday matters, but it is also invaluable for ministering. Whether you're doing one-on-one outreach, preaching, praying, or using spiritual gifts, you should always be listening for the voice of God. Someone may ask for prayer for a certain condition or situation, and before or during prayer, the Lord can speak to you and tell you the root of the issue.

An older preacher shared a funny story on this topic. He and his wife had been married several years. They had children who were now grown, and he and his wife were happily growing old together. One morning, his wife woke up feeling sick to her stomach. They did not have a lot of money and did not want to spend it on a visit to the doctor, so the old man knelt beside the bed where his wife was laying and prayed for her. As he tells the story, he began to rebuke the pain. He cursed the cause of the pain at its root and ordered the infirmity to leave her body immediately.

Within an hour his wife was feeling better. They thanked the Lord together and went about their day.

The next day, his wife woke up again feeling sick and had severe abdominal pain. Again, the old man prayed, but this time with more fervency. He said, "I speak to whatever is the cause of this illness and command you back to where you came." And again, within a matter of minutes, his wife began to feel better and gave glory to God. For the third time in as many days the same thing happened again. The old man was rather frustrated. He told his wife, "My love, I do not think this is an ordinary disease. I think it is a spirit of infirmity sent from hell. I have to rebuke that spirit in you."

The old preacher found his old, worn Bible, put on his white dress shirt, fetched his bottle of anointing oil, grabbed his handkerchief, and prepared to engage in spiritual warfare with that ol' menacing devil, satan himself. His poor wife could do nothing more but question how this spirit had gotten a hold of her and hope that her husband could rebuke this devil, so the pain would leave for good.

The old man was ready to begin casting out the devil when God spoke and said, "Do not say anything more! Take your wife to the doctor." The old man, recognizing the voice of God, obeyed and took his wife to the doctor that same hour, hoping that the doctor could explain what was happening.

They ran several tests on her, and after some time the doctor returned and said, "Reverend, congratulations! Your wife is pregnant!" (I'm laughing just writing the story.) The old preacher was dumbfounded. He did not know what to think.

He prayed and asked the Lord, "Lord, I cursed the disease, I ordered it to return to whence it came. When I decided it was a demon and had to rebuke him, why did you not tell me my wife was pregnant?"

The man said the Lord simply replied, "You did not ask me."

Ask, Then Wait

This anecdote is a humorous example of how we can rest in God's Word over our lives and rely on him to speak to us and lead us through every circumstance. We should all learn from this story and ask ourselves how much more effective our prayers could be if we prayed with revelation and understanding. We need to be sensitive to His voice; we need to move when he says, "Move," and stay still when he tells us, "Be still." We need to speak when He tells us to speak and keep quiet when He says to be silent.

I need to be able to hear his voice daily—not just when

I go to church. In no situation do you *not* need to hear God's voice. You need his voice at work and at home. Daniel never worked in a church, nor did Joseph, yet both of them shaped world history because they recognized and listened to God's voice. When you are at home with your family, is there any other place where you need God's voice more deeply? No honest parent would ever tell you they know exactly what they are doing or have figured out how to raise their children, but we have access to God's voice. God will guide you. He will teach you how to parent as he parents, and he will help you lead your children's hearts to him.

God is not only the God of ministers who work in churches, crusades, or missionary service, but he is also the God of all his children. It is all of God's children who need their Father's voice. When you learn to hear and follow God's voice, it will completely change your life. Do not waste another day living on your own without him speaking to you, but reach out to him right now and ask him what he has to say to you even in this very moment.

9

Our Calling

I've heard this verse quoted and used in sermons my entire life. Without a doubt, Acts 1:8 is one of the Pentecostal/ Charismatic movement's favorite passages of Scripture. The disciples waited in the upper room along with other believers for "the promise of the Father." Jesus said it would be "power," but what would it look like? How would they recognize it? Something new was about to happen to them, something worth waiting for. An empowerment was about to take place.

The Amplified Bible describes the word *power* found in Acts 1:8 as "ability/capability, efficiency, might." Using the description from the Amplified Bible, the verse could read, "You shall receive abilities that you have not had before, you will be efficient, and receive supernatural might when the Holy Spirit comes upon you!"

The initial upper room experience was more than a one-time religious event; it was the initial baptism of the

Holy Spirit that is now available to each and every believer today. Through the baptism of the Holy Spirit you have been given real, dynamic power, and Jesus said, "These signs shall follow them that believe" (Mark 16:17 KJV). This experience changes you.

A triumphant church understands its potential to be used by God through the power of the Holy Spirit and the gifts and abilities, which are at our disposal. The leading of the Holy Spirit should be evident in all aspects of our lives, salvation (see John 3:5–6; 14:18–20; Acts 1:5), daily living (John 16:13–15), prayer (Romans 8:26–27), and empowerment for ministry (Acts 1:8; 1 Corinthians 12:6).

We need to be filled—and stay full of the Holy Spirit. We must be steadfast and teach and preach about the Holy Spirit and the works of the Holy Spirit. We must continue to pray people through to their personal baptism of the Holy Spirit with the same passion of the early believers. We are called and labeled "Pentecostal" not because of doctrine, but because we have experienced Pentecost in our own lives.

We were admonished in Scripture to stay true to the doctrines and teachings of the apostles and prophets. Change is inevitable. Preferences in styles of music change every few years. We change or upgrade our buildings. At some point we went from pews to chairs, from hymnals to projectors, from song leaders to praise teams. Change is good and is inevitable. In the midst of change, some things must remain constant: our foundation must remain the same.

As a church, we evolve and adapt to changes in our world, but we cannot change the message of the necessity of being full of the Holy Spirit. There is something different about us that should be visible to everyone. Unbelievers, the religious world, and even the spirit world knows that there is something great and distinct about you and me.

That special quality or uniqueness is not because of something outward but is evidence of the empowerment you and I have received by and through the Holy Spirit. This precious gift of the Father has perpetual demonstration of evidence that will follow the believer as long as he or she stays filled with the Spirit. This endowment has given you God's power, and because of it you have supernatural abilities, and you will be efficient in what you do. You have divine strength to serve our Lord and Savior Jesus Christ.

The first-century church was Spirit-filled, Spirit-empowered, and Spirit-led. Through the power of the Holy Spirit, they were convincing in their speech. They operated in supernatural gifts and turned a group of believers into a force that turned their world upside down.

Their source was God, their dependency was on God, and their hope was built on nothing less. Their end game, their prize, was to see Jesus face to face. They counted it all as gain—both the good and the bad; it was all because of and for the cause of Christ. Consumed with Jesus, despite their shortcomings and inabilities, they became a supernatural force.

If this was true for them, it must be true for us as well. At this point in time, Christianity is the most persecuted religious group on the face of the earth. We've been ridiculed, and our identity has been marred by some, yet we still stand as the conduit by which Jesus wants to reveal himself to the world.

Our staunchest critics declare that Christianity is in decline, and our impact is waning, but even current research proves otherwise. The church of which Jesus Christ said, "The gates of hell shall not prevail" is still triumphant, still impacting, and still growing. Glenn Stanton of *The Federalist* reported on data compiled from Harvard University:

> Religious faith in America is going the way of the Yellow Pages and travel maps, we keep hearing. It's just a matter of time until Christianity's total and happy extinction, chortle our cultural elites. Is this true? Is churchgoing and religious adherence really in "widespread decline" so much so that conservative believers should suffer "growing anxiety"?
>
> Two words: Absolutely not.
>
> New research published late last year by scholars at Harvard University and Indiana University Bloomington is just the latest to reveal the myth. This research questioned the "secularization thesis," which holds that the United States is following most advanced industrial nations in the death of their once vibrant faith culture. Churches becoming mere landmarks, dance halls, boutique hotels, museums, and all that.

Not only did their examination find
no support for this secularization in terms
of actual practice and belief, the researchers
proclaim that religion continues to enjoy
"persistent and exceptional intensity" in
America. These researchers hold our nation
"remains an exceptional outlier and potential counter example to the secularization
thesis.[2]

To continue our legacy of being a triumphant church,
we learn from the mistakes and victories from generations
past. We contextualize that information in accordance with
our present generation's realities, and then, through the
guidance of the Holy Spirit, we find the place and role that
Christ has designed for us to play in his church.

We do all this in God's power, not in our own. We
work toward building God's kingdom in every area of society, wherever we find ourselves. He enables us to be his
witnesses who proclaim what we have seen and not just
what we have read, and then we perform signs and wonders
so that others may see and believe.

This is what we are called to in God's church. This is
the life available to you. The Holy Spirit is waiting for you.
Have you begun waiting for him to receive the promised gift
from the Father?

10

Many Members, One Body

Our heavenly Father's imagination is immense, and his creativity is so unique. Not only did he create the heavens and earth out of nothing, but he also created different types of creatures to inhabit the land and the sea, made every single snowflake different from one another, counted each grain of sand on the beaches and deserts, and created the color scheme he would use to paint all of his creation.

We have become new creatures: distinct and unique, different from one another not only in our DNA and physical attributes, but God has also made every one of our functions as believers unique. Each one of us serves a different purpose within the body of Christ. Although our ministries are distinct, he gave us the same purpose: to serve him as King and expand his kingdom.

Your life is not your own; it belongs to the Lord. Under the inspiration of the Holy Spirit, the apostle Paul wrote, "My old self has been crucified with Christ. It is no longer

I who live, but Christ lives in me. So I live in this earthly body by trusting in the Son of God, who loved me and gave himself for me" (Galatians 2:20 NLT).

God has called us from near and far, from different cultures and nationalities, from different languages and races—each of us with our own story, both men and women alike, to serve the King and advance His kingdom on the earth. We are not the same, but we have the same purpose. To each one "is given the manifestation of the Spirit for the common good" (1 Corinthians 12:7).

God has purposed that the working of the Spirit be manifest in your life, so that Christ is glorified, and the kingdom of God might advance. We must see ministry through this lens. The question should not be, "What do *I* profit from doing this ministry?" The correct question for right thinking is: "What is Jesus and the kingdom of God going to profit from this ministry?"

Not everyone is called to stand behind the pulpits of our churches. Not everyone can sing the solo, nor can we all be apostles, prophets, evangelists, pastors, or teachers. But every one of our lives has a specific plan and function that is divinely orchestrated and inspired by the Father, , so that Christ may be glorified, and the kingdom advance further. The early church honored its apostles, bishops, and elders, and it also understood that each believer was a witness of Christ to the world.

Do not despise where God has positioned you in the body of Christ. If you are called to be a "finger," do not waste time complaining that you are not an "eye." The eye may be seen as a more attractive member of the body, but imagine life without the ability to touch. If you have been positioned as one of the "feet" of the body, do not dwell that another may be called to function as an "arm." It may seem like an "arm" is stronger than a "foot," but on what would the body balance itself if not for feet? If the body of Christ had no "feet," how could it walk when the Lord says, "Go"?

I believe that each of us has been called to accomplish a task in the kingdom of God. We are fearfully and wonderfully made in the image of the Father, and each of us has a mission on earth just as Jesus did.

Knowing Your Place

I don't think there is a believer out there who hasn't had this thought: *I want to serve God, but I do not know how or where to serve.* I, for one, thank God people still want to serve him.

An eye-opening statistic came out several years ago concerning the church as a whole in North America. It was observed that only 20 percent of the members of the majority of Christian churches are involved in a ministry or serve in a specific role in their local congregation. The remaining four out of five people simply attend services and leave without further involvement.[3] Imagine for a moment the incredible growth and revival and how much more we could do if we could reverse that statistic. How many souls could be reached if 50 percent, 80 percent, or 90 percent of the membership understood that God has a specific purpose for them in the body of Christ and cooperated with God to carry out their ministry?

Understanding our function within the body of Christ is so crucial; it is important to us and the church at large. Take missions work for example. Matthew 24 says that when the gospel reaches every nation, *then* the end will come. Jesus is waiting for the church to share his good news with those groups who have not yet heard of him. Through Christian television, social media, and such, the gospel is reaching corners of the earth that, because of persecution or other difficulties, we have not been able to access.

Via the conduit of our giving and technological advances, each believer plays their part as a member of the body of Christ and the advancement of his kingdom on earth. Each one of us plays a role in spreading the gospel, and it's because of our collective efforts that many are still coming into the saving knowledge of the Lord Jesus Christ.

God doesn't waste a single one of his children. None of us is destined to sit on the sidelines, unable to do anything of benefit to his kingdom, but we have to understand that God's kingdom doesn't fit inside church buildings alone. Just as the church of God only meets in buildings we call "churches," the church of God cannot be simply reduced to how it expresses itself on Sundays.

Where does the church go all the other days of the week? It goes from the place where believers congregate to the places where unbelievers congregate: at work, school, shopping malls, grocery stores, and everywhere in between. These are exactly the places where the lost need believers to stand out and step into the power and wisdom of the Holy Spirit—to minister whenever and wherever possible. We need to ask the power of God to give us efficiency in our work and to make us stand out in our workplaces. We need to ask him to help us lead others both in the quality of work and toward the gospel.

Church on Sundays is certainly for worshiping God with fellow believers, but it is not limited to that. Church is for the equipping of the saints for the works of service (Ephesians 4:11–12). Those works of service are very much needed on Sundays and in church buildings, or in missionary service among the nations, but they are also needed in every single area of society.

God will not call every believer to full-time service in a church building. In fact, he will not call most believers to this. But God does call every believer to ministry, no matter who they are, where they work, where they live, what their family is like, whether they are men or women, boys or girls. God calls all his children to serve in his army, working to build his kingdom.

What role do you have in this work? It is not only important, but it is also necessary for you to fulfill your role. Press in to the Lord. Ask him to lead and guide you. You are God's child, and he did not create you or save you so that you could sit on the sidelines.

11

Healings and Miracles

I thank God for the gift and promise of healing for our bodies. The Lord Jesus declares, "They will be able to place their hands on the sick, and they will be healed" (Mark 16:18 NLT). Without question, it is God's will to heal. Not only is it his will, but he also wants to use you as an instrument to bring healing to the sick. The sacrifice of Jesus on Calvary bought us freedom from sin and condemnation, but it also bought healing of all sickness, disease, and pain. The early church fathers worked directly with Jesus in ministry and experienced firsthand how he ministered to individuals.

> That evening many demon-possessed people were brought to Jesus. He cast out the evil spirits with a simple command, and he healed all the sick. This fulfilled the word of the Lord through the prophet Isaiah, who

said, "He took our sicknesses and removed our diseases." (Matthew 8:1–17 NLT)

Surely he has borne our griefs and carried our sorrows; yet we esteemed him stricken, smitten by God, and afflicted. But he was pierced for our transgressions; he was crushed for our iniquities; upon him was the chastisement that brought us peace, and with his wounds we are healed.
(Isaiah 53:4–5)

The healing of the sick played a significant role in the ministry of Jesus Christ on earth. In Luke 4, Jesus, referring to the prophecy of Isaiah 61, said, "The Spirit of the Lord is upon me, because he has anointed me to proclaim good news to the poor. He has sent me to proclaim liberty to the captives and recovering of sight to the blind, to set at liberty those who are oppressed, to proclaim the year of the Lord's favor" (Luke 4:18–19).

Jesus' life and ministry of course was a fulfillment of ancient prophecies, including those pertaining to healing. With every individual who was healed and every miracle performed within his ministry, another prophecy was fulfilled to confirm that he was more than just a mere man; he was the Christ, the Messiah, who they had hoped and longed for.

Every Christian believes that Jesus, the Son of God performed miracles of healing and deliverance, but Jesus himself made it clear that his ministry of healing would not be unique to himself. In the Gospel of John, Jesus said, "Whoever believes in me will also do the works that I do; and greater works than these will he do" (14:12).

Through the access granted to you by the blood of Jesus and the authority of the Holy Spirit, you too can lay hands on the sick, and they shall recover. During his ministry on earth, we see that Jesus gave authority to his apostles and disciples to pray for the sick. In Matthew 10, Jesus commanded the apostles to heal the sick and proclaim the kingdom of God:

> Jesus called his twelve disciples to him and gave them authority to drive out impure spirits and to heal every disease and sickness ... "As you go, proclaim this message: 'The kingdom of heaven has come near.' Heal the sick, raise the dead, cleanse those who have leprosy, drive out demons. Freely you have received; freely give." (Matthew 10:1, 6–8 NLT)

In Luke, the command was given to the seventy believers to do the same:

> After this the Lord appointed seventy-two others and sent them two by two ahead of him to every town and place where he was about to go. He told them ... "Heal the sick who are there and tell them, 'The kingdom of God has come near to you.'" (Luke 10:1–2, 9 NLT)

As we read in the New Testament when Jesus ministered directly to a person, healing can come directly from God. Healing can be administered through the ministry, as shown by the ministry of the apostles. Healing can also be administered through believers, as shown in the sending of the seventy-two in Luke 11 and the charge of Jesus in Mark 16.

Healing and miracles are central not only to the ministry of Jesus but also to the ministry of the apostles. The anointing on Peter's life was so strong that some testified to being healed simply from his shadow passing over them. In earlier chapters we discussed how the sick people were laid out in the streets in hopes that Peter's shadow would pass over them and heal them. Peter and John raised up the crippled man who was right outside of the doors of the temple. Remember the anointing on Paul's life was such that people would touch cloths to his skin and bring them to the sick, and instantly the sick were healed.

At times, some have attempted to hijack this important ministry and corrupt it for personal gain while engaging in less than honest means. But their actions do not negate the necessity and role of healing within the church.

While facing a major battle against an illness that attacked a family member, a friend named Randy Hollis from Louisville, Kentucky, called me and said the following words that have never left me: "We have just as much right to the promise of the whipping post as we do the cross of Calvary!" He was saying that if we believe God for the salvation Jesus purchased on the cross, we should also believe God for the healing purchased in Jesus' stripes when he was whipped. Today, when I pray over the sick in crusades and in other places, I quote those words to remind us how much God wants us to prosper in health. By his stripes we *are* healed!

There are sicknesses simply brought on by life or as a part of life, but sicknesses can also be brought on by a spirit of infirmity. I tend not to give too much credit to the enemy, but we also must not be ignorant of his weapons or manners of attack in the battle for our salvation. The enemy can attack our bodies through sickness as seen in the life of Job, and the young boy the apostles prayed for whom they could not heal (Matthew 17:14–21).

The reasons for why the enemy would come against our health are quite obvious. His ultimate goals are to quench our faith in God, tire us until we can no longer fulfill our calling, and finally cause us to question God. Not every sickness is the result of the devil, but we recognize that some sicknesses are spiritual attacks.

Some years ago, I was invited to teach a seminar in South America in the country of Peru concerning the gifts of the Spirit and to conduct miracle-healing services during the evening. I was in good health, slept well, and arrived rested to the South American country. Within hours after arriving and checking into my hotel I became extremely sick and eventually bedridden for several days. I could not eat, my fever would not come down, and my body ached from head to toe. I can honestly say I have never been as sick as I was during that time. I was reluctant to visit a hospital in a foreign country, and I was traveling by myself. This was before we all had cell phones with international calling capabilities.

To make things worse, the delegation assigned to receive me at the airport and host me while in their city was unable to receive or host me due to a political protest that had taken place. The protesters had blocked the main streets leading into the mountainous city, and they could not get to me. I was alone and sick. There I was in a country to teach on the supernatural and conduct a miracle crusade, and I couldn't even get out of bed!

By coincidence, my father also happened to be in South America. He was preaching a crusade in the neighboring country of Colombia. I gave serious thought to trying to travel to my father. I wasn't able to call him, but I was tired, sick, and ready to see a familiar face that could help me. I gave thought to returning to the airport and simply going home, but I was even too weak to do that. I had already missed the first two days of services, and three were left to go, but there was no change in my condition.

Early one morning, there was a knock on my door, and then the door simply opened. In walked the bishop of the church of Peru. I had not spoken with him since my arrival in the country because I was so sick and because of the blockade into the city, which had apparently lifted since I was now seeing him in my room. He came next to my bed and said, "God brought you here for a divine purpose. This is an attack of the enemy. You cannot leave our country without ministering to us, and in Jesus' name I command this attack to come off you."

By lunchtime I was up and out of bed and able to eat for the first time in several days. By evening, my strength to minister was back—and did God ever move in those services!

God moved wondrously in those miracle services. In fact, in one of the most powerful examples of the gift of tongues I have ever experienced: An indigenous girl from the Andes Mountains spoke a word of knowledge directly from the Lord to me in perfect English. The enemy had intended to use this sickness or spirit of infirmity to drive me out of South America, but what the devil meant for evil, God used for good.

I have seen saints of God attacked by the spirit of infirmity and nearly lose their faith. They lead a healthy lives, eat right, sleep enough, and yet sometimes they cannot regain their health. They go to the doctor, and the doctor finds nothing wrong with them, or they take medicine that has no effect on them. When a natural cause cannot be found, it is my opinion that a spirit of infirmity may very well be at work.

Sickness is not always the result of the spirit of infirmity; rather, it is the result of us not taking care of ourselves. We get sick from simple things, like forgetting to washing our hands, or not eating right, or not getting adequate sleep. As much as we would like to blame the devil, some sicknesses are due to our own habits. And while it's obvious, it is also sometimes forgotten that some sickness and health struggles are simply part of our lives as humans on earth. I wish I could promise that every believer would never get sick or face a health challenge, but I cannot. Regarding sickness: While this is a subject about which many hundreds of books have been written, here is a summary of what I consider to be the two reasons for sickness.

Sicknesses to Manifest God's Works

As I said earlier in this chapter, health and healing played an important role in the ministry of Jesus Christ on earth. Healing and miracles were important components to proving he was the Messiah. When Jesus healed, he fulfilled prophecies, attracted more followers, and through the ministry of healing, signs and wonders were performed in front of unbelievers. Through the ministry of healing, many people came to know Jesus as both savior and healer.

One of the most effective tools of soul winning is a personal testimony of healing or a miracle. Why would God allow us to get sick? Why would he allow our bodies to be attacked? Jesus answered these specific questions:

> As he went along, he saw a man blind from birth. His disciples asked him, "Rabbi, who sinned, this man or his parents, that he was born blind?" "Neither this man nor his parents sinned," said Jesus, "but this happened so that the works of God might be displayed in him." (John 9:1–3 NLT)

Rather than call your sickness a curse and become bitter over it, speak healing in Jesus' name. When the healing comes, you will have obtained a testimony of personal healing that no one can take from you. The Bible says that we are made overcomers by the blood of the Lamb and *the word of our testimonies* (Revelation 12:11).

Your testimony of healing will increase your faith,

deepen your relationship with God, and make you a better witness of the power of God to the world. God will be glorified through his healing and miracle-working power.

Sickness unto Death

In the story of Lazarus, Jesus declared, "This illness does not lead to death. It is for the glory of God" (John 11:4). This is, at least to me, a confirmation that some sicknesses are meant "for the glory of God," or in other words, some sicknesses ultimately end in healing. Yet this could also be read that there are diseases and sickness that are unto death.

Unless the Lord comes first, we know that someday we will die. The Word says, "It is appointed to man to die once" (Hebrews 9:27). Dying is a natural occurrence of life. Death does not have to be the result of a lack of faith or an attack of the enemy. Every one of us will one day have an appointment with death unless the Lord comes first.

Having lost both my father and my late wife prematurely to illness, I feel that I have authority to speak regarding death. The pain of losing someone you love is difficult to express in words. The void is obvious and doesn't simply disappear. I hurt from the loss of my father and my late wife, yet at the same time I am able to be thankful because I believe that although they suffered with illness while here on earth, they are now both healed. Albeit not in the manner I may have wanted, but they are healed nonetheless. Upon his death, my father no longer needed a cane to walk, and his speech was no longer impeded as a result of illness, as it had been during the last year of his life. He was once again a strong man, a mighty man of God who was able to speak, sing, and worship along with the saints who had passed on before him.

Jessica, my late wife, battled leukemia for six months. She had literally gone through the fight of her life, and her body that had been ravaged with sickness bore the evidence of that battle. As difficult as it was to hold her as she breathed her last breath on the earth, I was also conscious that she was breathing her first breath of heaven's healing air. In an instant, she now stood in the presence of her Lord and Savior, healed and delivered from the curse of cancer.

I say all of this to say that death is painful for those of us who remain in the land of the living, but for a believer, even death is gain and brings healing. We are transformed! Eternal life is ours! That is why we can stand over the casket of a loved one and say, "O death, where is thy sting? O grave, where is thy victory?" (Hosea 13:14 KJV).

Remember, there is nothing impossible with God. We know that God can raise the dead or spare an individual who is near death. We know that He can heal any disease, but we also know that one day death will come to each of us. I do not question God as to, "Why did so-and-so die?" I know his thoughts and ideas are higher than mine. There are things I do not understand today, but if I could see eternity through the eyes of Jesus, and if I could look at things from the end to the beginning, maybe then I could understand God's plans.

12

Prayer: The Tool of Faith

If we are going to effectively function as the conduit of God's power, we must know how to pray. The most important part of praying is that we first must believe. He or she who prays must believe that God can heal, that God wants to heal, and that God can use him or her to pray for the sick.

In the description of the Great Commission found in Mark 16:16–18, the Lord commanded the believers to pray for the sick, and he promised to heal. Ask yourself these simple questions: Do you believe they are going to be healed? Do you believe God heard your prayer, and that the healing is taking place? And if not, how can you minister if you do not believe God is able?

When I pray for the sick, I do so with the certainty and expectancy that God wants to heal, and that he has placed his power in me (and you) to declare health. You must believe, by faith, that this power is in you. After having prayed for the sick and the person not being healed, I have heard many people say, "They didn't have faith." While that may be true, make sure *you* do! You need to make sure that *you* prayed in faith. The person who is praying is the source to whom the Lord releases his flow of power. Note how James describes the prayer for the sick as "the prayer of faith":

> Are any of you sick? You should call for the elders of the church to come and pray over you, anointing you with oil in the name of the Lord. Such a prayer offered in faith will heal the sick, and the Lord will make you well. And if you have committed any sins, you will be forgiven. (James 5:14–15, NLT)

It is good for the person who's receiving prayer to believe, but again, I place the responsibility on the person who's praying to stir up faith in the individual in need of healing. There are examples of some being healed without having first believed, and these were the miracles and healings that led them to Christ. The Lord blesses and moves according to our faith. In its simplest definition, faith means to believe or expect.

In the story of the pool of Bethesda, the Bible tells of a man who had been stricken with sickness for thirty-eight years. He had spent almost four decades of his life witnessing the miraculous and seeing God heal others while never experiencing healing himself. After all that time, while waiting for the angel of the Lord to stir and trouble the waters of Bethesda, the God that gave the angel the charge to stir the waters walked in, robed in the flesh. The visible image of the invisible God, Jesus Christ, walked into Bethesda and came to this man and asked if he wanted to be healed.

The answer seemed obvious. Of course, he wanted to be healed; he had laid poolside for thirty-eight years waiting for his moment of healing, yet when the Lord asked the question the man did not answer yes or no. Rather he spoke of all of those who did not help him with his miracle. There was no act of faith or even word of faith on his part. What was Jesus' response? He said, "Get up, take up your bed, and walk" (John 5:8).

The beggar's moment of healing had come, and even his lack of belief, or at least his inability to confess it, did not hinder what God had already ordained for him. That's good news for you and me. That reminds me that what God intends for my life, God will do.

You Have the Authority to Heal

Very few times in the Bible did God heal someone without having another human being pray for them. It does happen, but it is not as common. By God using a mere man or woman, he shows his power while also connecting the person with someone who can share the rest of the gospel with the individual. What this means is that you—yes, you—need to prepare yourself to see God work signs and wonders through your prayers. As you lay hands on people, you will see them recover.

I've heard it said somewhere that expectation is the

birthplace for the miraculous. Jesus made a similar statement to Martha in John 11:40: "Did I not tell you that if you believed you would see the glory of God?" This means that if you are going to pray for the sick, you need to believe they will recover when you do. You have to expect you will see the glory. Ask yourself, who has the authority to pray for the sick? If you are a believer, the answer is you. You can pray for the sick and see healing take place. Jesus promised, "These signs will accompany those who believe" (Mark 16:17). Every believer can lay hands on the sick, pray in faith, and declare healing.

In the Old Testament most healings and miracles came through a prophet. For example, Elijah healed the son of the widow, or Isaiah spoke life to King Hezekiah. In the New Testament, many were healed by Jesus, while others were healed by the apostles and disciples. For example (of course, there are many more):

- Peter heals the lame man at the temple gate (Acts 3).

- Phillip heals in Samaria (Acts 8:5–7).

- Ananias heals the eyes of Saul of Tarsus (Acts 9:10–18).

- Paul performs several miracles in Ephesus (Acts 19:11–12).

In these examples, only two in the list are known as apostles—Peter and Paul. Scripture tells us Phillip was an evangelist, but he started as simply a man who waited on tables to serve the widows their bread. Ananias, however, has no title given to him anywhere in Scripture other than "son of God" or "saint." If you believe in Jesus, you have these same titles, which is all you need to be qualified to work signs, wonders, and miracles in Jesus' name. Expect it and you will see it.

God Moves as He Pleases

I remember a certain occasion in our church in Virginia where the Lord chose to heal someone without human intervention. A newer convert brought her mother to one of our services. The mother of this recent convert had never attended a Spirit-filled church and wanted to see what her daughter had "gotten herself into."

The mother happened to suffer from a skin condition. Her arms were stained with discoloration. The lady never stood or moved throughout the service; she never reacted to the moving of the Spirit. But as I preached, the Lord decided to perform a sovereign act. During my message, this lady who did not participate in praise and who was skeptical of us was instantly healed of her skin disease. No one had prayed for her, no one laid hands on her; this was a sovereign act of God. While I was preaching, with great surprise, she told her daughter, "I do not know what just happened, but the stains are gone from my arms!" She was instantly healed and as a result believed in the Lord.

God moves and operates as he chooses to. He is God! While that is a simple statement, it is a statement we must believe. By declaring that he is God, we are declaring that he has sovereign power to use creation as he pleases for his glory.

It is true that there are some who seem to see more healing and miracles than others when they pray for the sick. I know men of God who it seems every time they minister, the sick are healed. First Corinthians speaks of a healing and miracle ministry. I believe the healing gift is a true, New Testament spiritual gift given to certain individuals in the body of Christ, and I still believe and recognize that any believer can lay hands on the sick and witness a healing take place.

> Here are some of the parts God has appointed for the church: first are apostles, second are prophets, third are teachers, then those who do miracles, those who have the gift of healing, those who can help others, those who have the gift of leadership, those who speak in unknown languages. (1 Corinthians 12:28 NLT)

We have more technology available to us than ever before, and we have more doctors than ever before. We've never been smarter or wiser than we are today, and yet we are ready to diagnose more sicknesses than ever before. There are pills for everything. I am not against medicine; in fact, I believe most of our medicine is another way God uses creation to heal or help us. He gave wisdom to the doctors and scientists to invent or discover these cures. Be it through the prayer of faith, or the assistance of medicine, or the workings of a doctor, God will always get the glory.

Praying for the Sick

We know that every believer has the ability, through the power of the Holy Spirit, to pray for the sick, and some among us have healing and miracle gifts. We must also know how to pray effectively. The healing ministry is not a science of precise formulas (other than to always pray "in Jesus' name"). In other words, there are many ways to pray for and minister to the sick. What I explain in this overview is what has been effective for me.

Pray: When I minister, I do not ask or beg God to heal the individual. Healing is a promise. This is the same thing we say to someone when we pray that they be filled with the Holy Spirit baptism. I don't beg for a gift; I claim it! I will say more about this in the next few pages that will make this clearer.

Environment: Create an environment of faith! Whether you are praying for an individual in a home, hospital, church service, or crusade, create an atmosphere and environment of faith. Exalt Jesus! Glorify Jesus! Talk about his wonders and power. Praise him, and faith will begin to rise around you and within you. Remember faith and expectation are the birthplaces for the miraculous.

Faith: Pray with faith and confidence. I believe that when I speak the word of faith, the sick will be healed. Praying with confidence is hard for many people because questions and doubts enter their minds: *What if the person is not healed? What if they do not get up? What will people think of me? What will my family think?* Let me "heal" you of doubt right now in Jesus' name and remind you of a very important principle: You do not heal the sick. God heals the sick.

That simple revelation or reminder should remove all the weight and pressure from your shoulders. You are the channel, the instrument, the vessel that God uses to transmit his Word and power to those who need it, but he is the one who does the work. If the Lord chooses to heal, it is his working, and he gets the glory. If the Lord chooses not to heal, it is his decision, and the glory is still his. You and I are merely the conduits by which he chooses to operate.

The Name: Always pray "in the name of the Lord Jesus Christ" and give God the glory. Colossians 3:17 says, "And whatever you do, in word or deed, do everything in the name of the Lord Jesus, giving thanks to God the Father through him." God does not and will not share his glory. Be sure that the person for whom you are praying is not putting their faith in you but in God. Remind them that God is about to touch them. Though your hand is on their forehead or body, the hand of the Lord is what will heal them.

Philippians 2:10 says: "So that at the name of Jesus every knee should bow, in heaven and on earth and under the earth, and every tongue confess that Jesus Christ is Lord, to the glory of God the Father." There is power in that name! Peter and John used that name in Acts 3, declaring to the lame man, "In the name of Jesus Christ, rise up and walk!" The matchless name of Jesus is wonderful! When you say that name, heaven stands to attention, God hears you, and miracles happen.

Direction: Speak directly to the disease or the part of the body that is afflicted and declare healing. When I pray, for example, for someone suffering from cancer, I speak the word of faith directly to their body or to the area of the body that's under attack by the cancer. I command the ruthless infirmity to leave and order the body be healed and restored. In the ministry of Jesus, we see him doing the same thing. If someone was dead, they were ordered to "awaken" or to rise up. To those who were blind, he commanded their eyes to be opened, and the lame to rise and walk. That same divine authority that was in Jesus is in us for we are the temple of the Holy Spirit.

When I'm in the will of God and living for the Lord, that authority is also within me to speak the word of faith and declare things that are not as though they were. Second Corinthians 4:13 says, "Since we have the same spirit of faith according to what has been written, 'I believed, and so I spoke,' we also believe, and so we also speak." Speaking of God, Paul says in Romans 4:17, "God ... who gives life to the dead and calls into existence the things that do not exist." This is the way God speaks: He creates things that previously didn't exist. He calls out to them as if they were, so that they suddenly spring forth. When we partner with God to bring healing to the sick, we speak in the same way. When I pray for the sick, I do not ask the Lord to heal them; I declare healing. I pray with faith and confidence. I give God the glory. I pray in the name of the Lord Jesus Christ. I believe they will be healed. And I pray believing that God is going to do the work.

Some years ago, I conducted a healing crusade in in the republic of El Salvador. A lady asked me to pray for her eyes because she was almost completely blind. She was led to me by a few of her friends, and it was obvious that her vision was impaired. I prayed for her and declared healing in Jesus' name. Upon praying for her, I asked if her vision had improved. To see if a healing had occurred, I stood a distance from her and asked her to mimic what I was doing.

I waved my hand at her and asked her to do the same back at me. It was quite obvious that she still could not see. She could not mimic me no matter how close I stood to her. I prayed for a second time, and nothing changed. I prayed a third time, and still nothing appeared to be changing for her, so I prayed one last time. This time her eyes were opened, and she was completely healed for the glory of God.

Laying on of Hands: It is biblical to lay hands on the sick. Many times, I lay my hands exactly on the part of the body or in the general area that is afflicted. If I am praying for someone's back, I put my hand on their back. If it is the leg, arm, or head, I do the same. Obviously, some areas are not appropriate to lay hands on, and in those cases I may simply lay hands on their head, shoulder, back, or whatever appropriate part of their body is nearest to the disease instead. I sometimes even have a person lay their hands on themselves on the afflicted area. Although Jesus didn't say we need to lay hands on the specific area, that is often my practice; he simply said that when we lay hands on the sick, they will recover.

Anointing Oil, Prayer Cloths, and Other Points of Contact: In the book of Galatians we read of anointing the sick with oil. There are several examples in the Bible of people being anointed with oil. Oil is symbolic of the Holy

Spirit and authority. Jesus anointed the sick, but it was never done the same way. He once used mud and saliva!

One of the reasons Jesus used different kinds of anointing or manners to pray for the sick was so that when the healing occurred, the credit for the healing or miracle would not be given to anything else but the Lord Jesus Christ. It wasn't a magic trick or potion that created the miracle, but it was the power of God. The power is not in the custom or manner in which we pray, but to whom we are praying.

In Acts 19:11 we read that "God was doing extraordinary miracles by the hands of Paul, so that even handkerchiefs or aprons that had touched his skin were carried away to the sick, and their diseases left them and the evil spirits came out of them." The handkerchiefs or aprons were points of faith or points of contact. The recipient of these items knew that the piece of cloth or apron had been with Paul, and that Paul had been with God. It was a point of contact that increased their faith. We do the same today. In a worship service where God is moving and people are being saved and healed, a person might ask for prayer for a relative who lives overseas.

Of course, it's not like I can leave the service immediately and fly to a far-off country to pray for the individual, but I can send my faith and prayer. I can pray over a cloth and send it to that person as a point of contact. Upon receiving it, the recipient of the point of contact receives more faith and, God willing, will be healed.

I believe we can see countless more miracles and healings by simply demonstrating our faith. Young children are known for wild imaginations and far-fetched dreams. Christ said that to enter his kingdom we must become as children again. Where are the dreamers among us? Where have the believers with child-like faith gone? It is they who I believe will see the miraculous in greater levels. They've read their Bibles, they've spent time with their Father, and they believe. Simply because they believe, they will see the glory of God.

Take the limits off God. Believe like never before that God can use you in the healing ministry. Pray for the sick. Pray until they receive healing. Then always give God the glory.

13

The Gifts of the Spirit

G od has given spiritual gifts to his church, empowered by the Holy Spirit, to minister to the body of Christ and to show God's power to the world. Each gift is unique and important. These nine gifts should always be in operation among us as we minister to one another and to unbelievers.

Is This Truly God?

Some believers have grown doubtful in accepting the gifts of the Spirit, and there are real reasons behind their apprehension. Their cynicism is normally tied to the misuse or abuse of the gifts of the Spirit. Some of this misuse has happened as people have counterfeited or imitated the gifts in order to manipulate people. Others, at times, have tried to obtain fame and attention through imitating spiritual gifts for an audience.

This has, of course, fostered pessimism among some

in regard to the gifts of the Holy Spirit, but it should not be this way. We are people of faith who believe in the supernatural. The God who robed himself in flesh and healed many in Jerusalem and sent the angel to trouble the healing waters of Bethesda is the same God who heals today. Simply because some have perverted the gift does not mean the gift no longer exists in its true form from God. Should we stop using God's gifts rightly just because some have used them wrongly? Of course not!

And how can we believe that God will fill a person with the Holy Spirit and cause them to speak in other tongues but not believe in the gift of prophecy or the gift of knowledge? Nothing counterfeit could exist if the truth—something genuine—did not exist first. The enemy of our souls wants us to doubt the supernatural power of God. He desires that we be people who are hesitant to believe and who do not lead lives of faith.

We must remember who we are: We are people of faith. We serve a God who does extraordinary things. God has given us analytical minds and powers of reason, but he has also revealed his mighty power for us to see and enjoy. If you have faith, God can use you in supernatural dimensions for his glory.

Introducing Spiritual Gifts

Paul told the Corinthians that he did not want the to be unaware or ignorant of spiritual gifts, so we should not be ignorant about them either. I will teach you about all nine gifts Paul mentions in 1 Corinthians 12, but it is important to emphasize what Paul first says about them:

> To each is given the manifestation of the
> Spirit for the common good. For to one is
> given through the Spirit the utterance of
> wisdom, and to another the utterance of
> knowledge according to the same Spirit, to
> another faith by the same Spirit, to another
> gifts of healing by the one Spirit, to another
> the working of miracles, to another proph-
> ecy, to another the ability to distinguish
> between spirits, to another various kinds
> of tongues, to another the interpretation of
> tongues. All these are empowered by one
> and the same Spirit, who apportions to each
> one individually as he wills. (1 Corinthians
> 12:7–11)

Here, he lists nine different gifts of the Holy Spirit, saying that each one is given to some believers in the body of Christ, but there is something that unites them all, and in uniting the gifts, it unites us in one body under Christ Jesus. He says, "To each is given the manifestation of the Spirit for the common good" (12:7).

This tells us two important things. First, we know that each gift is a manifestation of the same Spirit—the Holy Spirit. Therefore, we should not worry about the gifts coming from any demonic source or be distracted, as the

Corinthians were, by the thought of each gift coming from a different angel. No matter the gift, no matter how it works through different ministers, they are all different ways the Holy Spirit reveals himself to us. In this way, each unique revelation brings glory to God.

Secondly, no matter the gift, they all serve the same general purpose: "For the common good." Paul later hammered on this truth with an entire chapter focused on love being at the heart of every gift. Gifts are not for elevating ourselves, growing our ministries for our own name's sake, manipulating people through power, or for any purpose other than the common good. Some have used gifts of the Spirit before to publicly humiliate people by revealing their private sins or family struggles. This certainly revealed the power of God, but not his love with it, so it wasn't for the common good and was instead an abuse of the gift entrusted to those ministers. If it isn't working good for someone, it isn't a rightly used gift of the Holy Spirit.

As Paul spoke this before listing any of the gifts, these two things are true for all of them. Now, to understand each individual gift, we start with words of knowledge.

Word of Knowledge

The word of knowledge is a revelatory gift, meaning that it is revelation of facts either past or present. If you want to be effective in God's work, it is helpful to know what you're working with, and the revelatory gifts can be tricky to keep straight because they are so similar.

My prayer and ministry can be more effective because

the word of knowledge can reveal the root of the problem or situation. Through the word of knowledge, someone's name whom you did not know previously may be revealed to you, or a situation or condition that someone has been suffering in private that God wants to heal or deliver them from becomes revealed to you.

I was teaching a group of pastors and ministers at a seminar in Guatemala on how to pray for the sick. It was not a worship service, healing crusade, or anything similar. It was just a teaching seminar. I asked for a volunteer to come forward whom I could use as an example of how to pray for the sick. I had never met the man who came forward. When he came forward, I continued my example and said, "Let's assume that this man has a heart condition, let's assume he has an irregular heartbeat, and he's just gone to the cardiologist and did not receive a good report."

I was using this simply to explain how I would pray for a person in that condition. No sooner had I said the last sentence when the man began to weep. I laid hands on this man as part of my example on how to pray for the sick to show the group how I would pray. When I laid my hand over his heart, the man fell to the floor slain in the Spirit. I had a few men pick him up, and as he stood, he rose up glorifying God.

Let me remind you, we were in a seminar, which is typically not the place where you would expect a wonderful interruption like this. I attempted to calm the man down and understand what had happened to him. The man said, "Oh, God is good! Before coming to the seminar, I went to the cardiologist, and he told me I had an irregular heartbeat, and there was not much he could do about it."

Was this a coincidence? I don't think it was. In the middle of a seminar where I needed a volunteer to demonstrate how to pray for the sick, the Lord gave a word of knowledge, and by that word, God was glorified once again. The gifts of the Spirit are for the edification—not the destruction of a person's faith. God is not going to reveal something to you that will bring shame to someone. Beware of people who insinuate or pretend they know something, when in fact, God has said nothing to them at all.

Some people masquerade as spiritual beings, and they try to use the gifts, such as the word of knowledge to manipulate others. They use scare tactics and say they see dark clouds, or they talk of death all the time. They ask you many questions, and then say God told them the same. If God has spoken it to them, then why did they have to ask? We have a lot of "fishermen" out there "fishing" for information that they later present as words of knowledge.

Sometimes, you may see that someone can discern accurate information about a person, but it is not by the Spirit of God. It's important to know that accuracy is not necessarily a sign that a gift is from God; the fruit of the gift is the sign that it's from God. Does it lead people to salvation in Jesus? Does it set the person free in truth? Does it lead to the glorification of God? These are questions we must ask. We can see from the story of the Philippian girl who followed Paul and declared true words of knowledge about him by a spirit of divination that accurate words are not always from the Holy Spirit.

If you cannot tell whose power is behind the word of knowledge by using these questions, God has also given us the ability to discern spirits. His Spirit will confirm whether what is happening is from God or not. If you are unsure, talk to your pastor, spiritual covering, or elder and seek further confirmation.

There is no need to fear words of knowledge from a demonic spirit. If you pursue the Lord, you will only hear from the Lord. And, usually, if you are hearing words of knowledge given in a church context, especially from already trusted and established leaders, you will see the answers to those questions quickly and easily.

Word of Wisdom

While the word of knowledge reveals the facts (past or present) of a problem or situation, the word of wisdom reveals the solution to the problem, or in other words, gives us the "what to do" with the facts presented.

The word of wisdom gift works hand in hand with the word of knowledge. What profit is there to tell someone their problem and not offer a solution to their problem? I still am in awe of God when he brings instruction and wisdom to us through another person who does not know what we are going through. If you are in a position that involves counseling as part of your job description, it is good to pray and ask the Holy Spirit to give you the word of wisdom gift. Instead of being quick to speak, meditate on the Lord and await the word of wisdom. The word of wisdom does not always make sense to us, but whether I understand it or not, I must obey the word. If the word is for someone I am ministering to, I speak the word to them and then obey the word of the Lord.

In reference to these two particular gifts—to be used in the word of knowledge and the word of wisdom—you must learn to listen to and know God's voice. You must know when and how God speaks to you. These are "revelatory gifts," and God uses different means to bring revelation. He may choose to speak to you directly in an audible voice, or he may choose to give you a vision. You may feel something in your body, or words may come to your mind. God reveals information to us in many ways. Be sensitive to God.

Listen for that still small voice that encouraged Elijah while hidden the cave, or look to see something, or pay attention to feel something. I know few people who hear an audible voice every time they minister. When we say, "God is speaking to me," many times we are referring to God speaking to our heart. It is as if one hears a voice from within speaking to one's mind or one's heart.

In closing on this subject, remember the gifts of God do not bring fear; they bring peace. The gifts of God do not bring more confusion, they bring truth which brings resolution. If you are ministering to someone, and you feel you have a word for them that you know would be confusing or bring them fear, go back to the Lord with it to dig deeper into what he may be telling you. Keep asking God what he wants to do or say until you have confidence that the word will bring peace and clarity.

Gift of Faith

Faith is not only a gift of the Spirit but is also listed as a fruit of the Spirit as well (Galatians 5:22). Some people bring so much encouragement and inspiration that no matter what type of problem or situation you are going through, you have more faith and hope simply after being with them. The gift of faith is the ability to raise the expectations of others and make them believe in God for greater things. Every believer has a measure of faith but should also seek to minister and operate in the gift of faith, so that when you speak as an oracle of the Lord, what you speak comes into existence.

It is by the gift of faith that we declare the works of the Lord done, even before seeing evidence that the work has been completed. The Bible says we must possess faith to please God. With that said, let me also add that we must have faith to have results in ministry. God is moved by and responds to faith. Faith is the currency of the kingdom of God. If you can believe that nothing is impossible for God, then you will see the impossible become possible. We must raise the level of expectation of the people we minister to, so they believe that God wants to do something supernatural in our midst. I am certain we will see an increase of miracles and healing and experience more supernatural visitations if we would believe and declare that every time we meet is an opportunity to see a miracle.

I believe there are levels of faith that begin with the simple belief in God. Belief rises to hope, and hope rises to great faith, but there is a level, which I believe is the highest level of faith, called expectation. I was always attracted to the supernatural and hungered to see more of it. I would listen to missionaries tell of what they were seeing in foreign countries, and I would jealously dream of it happening in our home church. I didn't want to simply read or hear about miracles; I wanted to see them come to pass here and in our time!

In an earlier chapter, I mentioned my experience in learning expectancy at a healing crusade in Chicago in the late '90s. I was hungry for more of the Lord and what he was doing. At this crusade, I saw people stand up and walk away from their wheelchairs. I was watching a dream become a reality. Things I had only heard of were now happening right before my eyes. I was overwhelmed by what God was doing. The preacher had yet to preach. This was happening during worship.

Praise and worship produces faith because it sets our attention and focus on God. The Bible tells us that God inhabits the praise of his people. The fullness of the Godhead, along with his blessings and benefits, fill the earth when his praise and worship comes from the earth. It serves as a magnet and brings heaven to the earth. When God shows up, he never leaves a place or person the same.

The same shekinah glory that filled the tabernacle of Moses consumed the sacrifices of Abraham, Elijah, Elisha, David, Samuel, and so many great prophets and patriarchs. The same Spirit that raised Jesus from the dead fills us and the places we are in when we praise the name of the Lord.

Are you in a situation where you need God to show up immediately? Praise him!

Are you going through a situation and just don't know what to say? Praise God.

Cause heaven to come to the earth through praise, and watch and see what happens when God shows up.

Overwhelmed by what I was seeing, I stepped outside of that arena and paced the lobby as I took everything in that I was seeing. There were well over ten thousand people who had gathered. The stadium was filled to capacity, yet I noticed that there was still a line of people standing outside trying to get in the stadium only to be turned away by the stadium's management due to seating regulations.

This is the same situation I mentioned earlier in this book, but this is such an important principle that I want to remind you. One woman begged and pleaded to get in. She was yanking on the door and trying to pull it open, and I heard her say to the security agent "Let me in! Let me in! If only I could get into the stadium I know I will be healed! Let me in!" She wasn't hoping for a miracle. She wasn't praying for a miracle. She was expecting a miracle. She was convinced that if she could just step into that place she would receive the healing she sought.

She reminded me of the woman with the issue of blood. While the multitude gathered and waited for a touch from Jesus, the woman with the issue of blood said, "I've waited too long, and I've suffered too long; I'm going to touch him. I know what happens when Jesus enters a city; I know what happens when he prays for the sick. I'm going to touch him, and I know that I will be healed." That's expectation!

I was immediately convicted as I sat and watched what was taking place at that crusade. I wondered if anyone had ever attended our church with such faith that they were convinced if they could just step on the property or walk into the sanctuary, they would be healed. I wondered if I had ever possessed that kind of faith?

Many times, we come to the Lord hoping for a miracle with our fingers crossed, when the correct approach is to come expecting—with hands wide open to receive. God responds to that kind of faith! What would happen to our local churches if people came to Sunday worship service with the same mentality as the woman turned away from the stadium? Every service, every time we gather in worship—be it two people or more—is an opportunity for the miraculous to take place. It is our duty to create an atmosphere of faith in every service.

That woman's display of faith changed me. From that point forward, I've always come to the Lord expecting—not merely hoping. When I pray, I expect that he will answer. When I need an answer, I expect the answer will come. That woman's faith changed my life.

In the dimension of expectation, my actions and words must come into alignment. I take acts of faith based on my expectation that God will do what only he can do. As believers and ministers, our words should always be "faith words." I want to speak life, healing, hope, love, and mercy. I want the people I talk to and interact with to bear witness to the Spirit of God living inside of me. I don't want to be guilty of speaking negatively. I don't want to be guilty of acting reluctantly but rather in faith. Speak faith! Act in faith! And watch heaven come to earth!

Gift of Healing

This is the ability to call on the name of Jesus and see the sick healed for the glory of God. To operate in this gift, you must have compassion for the sick, and you must have faith that God can heal any person of any infirmity. As I mentioned in the chapter on healing, we all have the ability to pray for the sick and see God heal them. This is one of the signs that follows believers, but 1 Corinthians also mention the gift of healing. One of the most obvious signs of this gift is that the sick are consistently healed when you pray. Not everyone has to be healed for you to know you have this gift, but there will be strong evidence of healing taking place as you minister.

The more you can believe, the more you will see. When operating in this gift, remember that God is the healer, and you are his instrument or vessel. Speak words of healing to the sick by faith in Jesus' name. Healing is not always going to be instantaneous. You can pray for the sick today and not see the result of the prayer for several weeks, but when that person is healed, they will remember the prayer of faith that you spoke and know that this was the work of God. Jesus said to Mary and Martha that Lazarus' sickness would be "to the glory of God," yet he was not instantly healed. He was, however, healed when he was raised from the dead, and this miracle resulted in many coming to believe in Jesus.

Working of Miracles

When speaking of sickness or physical needs, the difference between the gift of healing and the gift of miracles is that miracles are instantaneous. Healing is a process of time whereas the miraculous can take place in a moment. For example, if I pray for a person who is in a wheelchair, and they immediately rise up and walk, we've just seen a miracle. It's common to call healings miracles and vice versa. I do not think it really matters what you call it as long as Jesus gets the glory.

Miracles are not relegated to only physical needs either. There are financial miracles and many other examples. Our God is a God of wonders, the Great El Shaddai, which translates "Great God Almighty," and he enjoys working miracles and demonstrating his power. He delights in showing you his power. I encourage you to ask the Lord to show His miraculous power in your church and your life.

Gift of Prophecy

Paul wrote three chapters of 1 Corinthians just to talk about spiritual gifts, but the third chapter talks almost exclusively about two of them: prophecy and speaking in tongues. He starts by saying, "Pursue love, and earnestly desire the spiritual gifts, especially that you may prophesy ... the one who prophesies speaks to people for their upbuilding and encouragement and consolation" (1 Corinthians 14:1, 3).

The gift of prophecy is so powerful in communicating God's love that Paul says we are to desire it above all the other gifts. The definition of prophecy I was taught and still use today is "to speak by divine influence; speaking of things that are or are to come." This is fairly obvious and straightforward. None of the gifts can be used without divine influence, meaning that we cannot do them without God's empowerment. However, once God empowers us with those gifts, many of them can be used whenever we choose to use them. Speaking in tongues and prophesying are both examples of this. If we have received these gifts, we simply lean our hearts toward what God is saying and trust him to speak through us.

Prophecy speaks the word of God to build people's lives, encourages them, or comforts them, as Paul wrote to the Corinthians. It does this by revealing wonderful things God has put inside them, declaring the future to them, and revealing God's heart about either them or their circumstances. When I speak or preach under the anointing and authority of God, I can prophesy. This happens frequently then I am pressing into the Spirit of God during meetings. I want to declare his word to the people and sometimes he will then give me a specific word for a specific individual, corporate gathering, or city. As you press into the Lord, he will speak to you as well.

When you prophesy, you testify to the power of Jesus. You are putting the word of God into action. John 1:1 says, "In the beginning was the Word, and the Word was with God, and the Word was God" (NIV). While that is true and is a favorite verse of believers as written in English, I personally like the Spanish version of John 1:1 much better. It says, "In the beginning was the verb, the verb was with God, and the verb was God!" A verb, as you know, is not simply a spoken word but it is a "word in action." Jesus Christ is more than just a word; he is the ultimate verb. He is his "Word in action!" A prophetic word is a living word. It cannot return void; it is, "yes and amen," and it shall come to pass.

The Gift of Prophecy and the Ministry of a Prophet

Giving a prophetic word does not automatically make one a prophet. There is a difference between the gift of prophecy and the office (or ministry) of the prophet. God can use any believer to give a prophetic word to encourage or comfort another person, while the prophet's ministry does those same things in addition to bringing direction and revelation to the church. Both the gift of prophecy and the office of a prophet are important, but neither of them should make us feel arrogant. Remember that what God is doing through you is because of the anointing and the power of the Holy Spirit.

Before every crusade or healing service I minister in, I remind myself: Before God used me, he had already used a donkey to speak to and correct a prophet. But Balaam's donkey had no right to get puffed up either because before God used a donkey, he spoke to Moses through a burning bush. And before the bush declares it is the only way God can speak, the bush must remember that God spoke when there was only darkness, causing the universe to burst into existence. It's not us doing the work; it's him.

Discerning Spirits

"Beloved, do not believe every spirit, but test
the spirits to see whether they are from God,
for many false prophets have gone out into
the world." (1 John 4:1)

Discerning of spirits is another revelatory gift that every believer should be sensitive to, especially in our day and age. The cultures we live in are very curious about the supernatural, and the devil knows it. There is a hunger amongst mankind to find something bigger than ourselves. For people not looking to God, the devil has tried to simulate and mimic the supernatural power of God.

The enemy's goal has always been the same: to rob God of the glory due to Him. Satan has worked in the world by convincing people that there is power in crystals, nature, rocks, salts, spirits, and more. I believe hell has created the recent curiosity in angels, spirits, witchcraft, magic, and anything else with power that doesn't glorify Jesus.

We must discern these evil spirits and immediately take authority in the name of Jesus. The devil is the master of deceit. He goes as far as hiding behind the veil of religion. His deceptive nature is such that when he realizes that he cannot bind you with things of this world, he will attempt to bind you using religion:

> These people are false apostles. They are
> deceitful workers who disguise themselves
> as apostles of Christ. But I am not surprised!
> Even Satan disguises himself as an angel of
> light. So it is no wonder that his servants
> also disguise themselves as servants of righ-
> teousness. (2 Corinthians 11:13–15 NLT)

Religion is not necessarily a bad thing. James tells us there is a kind of religion that is pure and undefiled in God's sight (James 1:27). However, religion that is a tool of satan is any religion that teaches people to strive and labor to prove themselves to God. Demonic religion focuses on how people are sinful or evil, and it prescribes rituals, self-denial, and sacrifices as the means of making things right. We can do all those things and make them look Christian, but they can be completely empty of power and do nothing to make us like God.

Our hope is not in rituals and self-sacrificing efforts, but in Jesus' blood shed for us. We can never accomplish enough on our own to make ourselves good enough, but Jesus is willing and able to make us completely new creations, not through our efforts, but through faith. Any religion that denies Jesus' lordship and supremacy over all is a false religion, even if it has the trappings of Christianity.

We can recognize some of this because we understand these truths, but sometimes it can be difficult to see. That is why we need the discernment of spirits. This gift can help you see or feel the difference between God's true light and satan's imitation light. Also, there are false prophets in the land, speaking, prophesying, and giving the appearance that they are of God, but through the discernment of spirits we know that they are not of our kingdom. The operation of this gift is so important to me that I will not minister in any conference, crusade, or country without first asking God to give me the discernment of spirits; in Matthew 7, Jesus says:

> "Not everyone who calls out to me, 'Lord! Lord!' will enter the Kingdom of Heaven. Only those who actually do the will of my Father in heaven will enter. On judgment day many will say to me, 'Lord! Lord! We prophesied in your name and cast out demons in your name and performed many miracles in your name.' But I will reply, 'I never knew you. Get away from me, you who break God's laws.'" (Matthew 7:21–23 NLT)

When we speak of the prophetic ministry and the gifts of the Spirit, we speak much about the emphasis on faith, having an open mind, and taking limits off God. While those things are necessary and true, you must also be alert and discerning, recognizing that the devil comes to kill, steal, and destroy.

The Bible admonishes us to "test the spirits." If you are not sure if someone or something is of God, pray and talk to your pastor or elder. Remember that God does not bring confusion; he brings truth. Nothing and no one should take the glory from God.

Diverse Kinds of Tongues and Interpretation of Tongues

As I said before, the Lord uses different ways to speak to his people. When God spoke to Moses there was no need to use a burning bush, but God really wanted to get Moses' attention and give him a sign of the miracles that would become commonplace as he led the children of Israel out of captivity. There was no need for Jesus to put mud on the eyes of the blind man in John 9, but the Lord was testing the man's obedience to his word. There are many ways God speaks, and he has his reasons for choosing to speak those "languages" when he uses them. One of these extraordinary ways in which the Lord speaks is through the gift of tongues.

The gift of diverse kinds of tongues is different than the evidence of tongues one experiences when one is baptized in the Holy Spirit. Everyone can receive the Holy Spirit with the evidence of speaking in tongues, but not everyone has the gift of diverse kinds of tongues. I have combined the gift of diverse kinds of tongues with the gift of interpretation in this section because it is difficult to talk about one without talking about the other. These two gifts work hand in hand.

When a word from God comes through the gifts of tongues and the interpretation of tongues, it has usually been to confirm or reaffirm something prophesied or preached, yet it is not the only way the two gifts operate. I have been in prayer services where the two gifts operated, and the message was of direction for a church or a particular person. Speaking in tongues is God speaking directly to his people. It is noteworthy when God will speak through tongues and interpretation of tongues, therefore we must pay attention.

I was in a bilingual service some years ago in which a message in tongues was given. I quickly picked up my microphone thinking that most likely the interpretation would come in English and I would have to translate into Spanish. God did something that day that I've never seen him do before or since. After the message was given in tongues, a Hispanic woman raised her voice and began to give the interpretation in Spanish, and as she finished another woman raised her voice and gave the same interpretation in English.

It was exactly the same! The women who gave the interpretation in English did not speak Spanish and therefore could not have understood the first interpretation. God had given the same interpretation to two people speaking two different languages so that all the people gathered in that service would understand the word of God. If there was any doubt in my mind before that day concerning the gifts of tongues and interpretation of tongues, it went away.

First Corinthians gives much instruction on how to maintain order in our services. As I have stated several times, there is no science to the move of the Spirit. God speaks and uses each one of us in different ways. How do you know what gift the Lord wants to use you in? I think that with every gift, the initial sign that the Lord wants to use you is the inexplicable impulse you feel when you are supposed to do something at that particular moment. Expectation is where it all starts.

14

The Operation of the Gifts

Paul devoted an entire chapter to explain the gifts of God to the church and another to explain the operation and order of those gifts. Like Paul, I've given a brief explanation of each gift in this book; now I want to establish how those gifts should operate in the body of Christ.

The gifts of the Spirit are to minister to both the lost and the saved and to bring glory to God. They are not for us to boast on how God uses us, but that God might be glorified. You will be used in the gifts of the Spirit to do the work of the King and advance his kingdom. Before you minister to someone, it is important to check what your motives are. Above all else, our motive should be to bring glory to God and the name of Jesus Christ.

To do that, you must make sure that you are operating in the love of Christ. God has called us to heal, not hurt, and for that reason we must minister with compassion. There is no text book to explain exactly how to operate in the Spirit, but certain things must be in order. We must have compassion for the people or person we are ministering to. We must be humble before God, faithful, obedient, and submitted to the authority God has placed over us. We minister by and through faith—we must believe. If we try to analyze everything and come up with logical explanations and conclusions we will lose the element of faith necessary to flow in the Spirit.

Test the spirits and make sure God is leading you. If God is in it, the person will be healed, lifted up, and encouraged, and Christ will be glorified. If the spirit guiding you or speaking to you is not of God, it will bring confusion, shame, false doctrine, and doubt, and the focus will be more about man than of God.

You are the vessel that God will use to do his work on earth. Remove all your doubts and excuses for why you think God can't use you. The work that God is going to do through you will not be because you are good but because God is good. You are simply the channel or vessel that is going to be used.

I remind myself while I am ministering, that it is not I who is speaking, but God is speaking though me. I do not want anything to interfere with my connection with God; my focus is only on the Lord. I create an atmosphere or environment of faith in me first, then I transfer that faith to others. If I do not believe God can and will do the miraculous, the people I am ministering to will not believe God can do the miraculous.

I take the initiative to worship God before the music starts. God moves in the midst of the praises of his people, and if I want to be a part of the movement of God, I must be a worshiper. Read that carefully: I must be a worshiper. That does not mean I sing simply when the music plays, but it means my heart is toward God with an attitude of worship at all times—especially before I step forward to minister.

In a movement of God, it is easy to say, "I could not control myself," but 1 Corinthians 14:32–33 says, "And the spirits of prophets are subject to prophets. For God is not a God of confusion but of peace." When God's power moves upon you, it can be powerful. This can lead to us thinking we have no choice in the matter of what happens, but we always have the choice to wait for the right time.

The Corinthians would all blurt out their tongues or prophecies all at the same time, and it brought such chaos that it prevented anyone from benefiting from the gifts as God intended. God is not glorified in such a practice. We must do things decently and in order, so the gift serves its purpose, and God receives the glory. I remind you again that all we say or do is to glorify Jesus Christ.

The gifts of the Holy Spirit are for the edification of the body of Christ, not the destruction of the body. God is not going to give you revelation or a word that destroys the faith of others. Jesus Christ is a gentleman. He does not disappoint people nor should we embarrass people. Jesus ministered because he was moved with compassion, and in the same fashion, we should be moved with compassion.

When you first begin to minister and operate in the gifts of the Spirit, it is important to stay close to your pastor or elder, so they can mentor you. If you feel that you have seen, felt, or heard something from God, seek confirmation from your pastor or elder before sharing it. If what you feel is of God, God will confirm it through your pastor or mentor. If your pastor or elder does not confirm that what you felt is of God, respect their counsel and leave it alone. If what you felt was truly of God then, as is it written, "Heaven and earth pass away, but my words will not pass away" (Matthew 24:35). If what you felt is of God, God will bring his word to come to pass.

If you give a prophetic word, there is one specific and important instruction for ensuring it is in order: the word must be judged. Paul wrote, "Let two or three prophets speak, and let the others pass judgment" (1 Corinthians 14:29 NASB). The phrase "pass judgment" is so anti-grace that most don't like to use it, but it is what Paul called for us to do. The prophetic words were judged to be of God or not by the prophets, according to Paul. The judgment simply means they were to make a distinction whether the word was from God or not. It's interesting that in the Old Testament, the only way to test a word was to see if it came to pass, but in the New Testament and because God has given his Spirit to all believers, we are able to test the words people declare and determine whether or not they are from God.

This distinction helps maintain decency and order when our churches operate in the gifts of the Holy Spirit. The gifts of the Spirit cannot flow in chaos, or at least they cannot fulfill God's purpose for them or bring him glory. God is not the author of confusion. When God comes, he establishes order. When order leaves, I believe the movement of the Spirit can be quenched.

Boldness

Ministry requires boldness. I remember one of the first times that God used me in the gift of healing. I prayed for a young man who was crippled and required a crutch to walk. He approached the altar, dragging his leg. I prayed for him in the name of Jesus, declared healing, and in a moment of faith, I took the crutch—hoping and believing to see a miracle. Instead of walking or running on a brand new leg by the power of God, the boy tumbled over and fell in front of everyone still crippled.

In seconds, I had to decide whether to go running out the back door embarrassed at what had just taken place or be bold and still have faith that God would heal the boy. It required boldness. I looked at the boy lying on the floor, I held out my hand and said, "In the name of Jesus, get up and walk!"

He had already fallen once, there was no physical evidence that something had changed in him, but boldness came over me. For the glory of God, that boy stood up, and when he got up, his leg, which was twisted and lame, straightened completely out. He walked around the platform for a while and then began jumping and running, completely healed by the power of the Lord Jesus.

What would've happened if I would not have reached out to the boy a second time? What if I had left him lying on the floor? Faith ministry is saying and doing things without any proof or evidence. Think for a moment of the request made by Joshua to the Lord when the Israelites defeated the Amorites. His people were in battle, and the sun was about to set. In a moment of extraordinary boldness and faith, "Joshua prayed to the Lord in front of all the people of Israel. He said, 'Let the sun stand still over Gibeon, and the moon over the valley of Aijalon'" (Joshua 10:12 NLT). Joshua's request makes no scientific sense, as we now know, but verse thirteen says that what he spoke is exactly what happened: "So the sun stood still and the moon stayed in place until the nation of Israel had defeated its enemies" (NLT).

The sun and the moon stopped because Joshua had the faith to ask it or speak it. The Lord was moved by the faith of Joshua, and although what he was asking for was not logical or scientifically correct, God did it simply because Joshua had the faith to ask for it and speak it. There are things I do not understand; there are diseases that I do not understand, but what I *do* understand is that prayer is effective, and God hears and answers our prayers. Take the limits off God!

Most of the gifts of the Spirit are "speaking gifts," meaning that you need to hear from God to use them. The more time I spend in ministry, the more I learn that to be truly effective we must talk less and listen more. You cannot speak a word of knowledge, word of wisdom, or prophesy unless you have first heard a word from the Lord. Your job is to always be listening to for his voice and be ready to respond when he speaks to you.

If you are not sure what God is saying, do not say, "God told me" or "Thus says the Lord." It is much better to say, "I think I feel this word for you from the Lord." No one likes to have someone speak in their name and associate quotes or promises to them that they never said. How much more is that true of our God? When you have said, "Thus says the Lord," the recipient of that word believes that what you are speaking is going to come to pass because, after all, it was a thus-says-the-Lord word. When it doesn't come to pass, you risk severe damage to that person's walk with God and their faith.

God is a gentleman, and you need to be a gentleman or a gentlewoman. God will never use you to embarrass a person. The gifts of the Spirit are for the edification of the body of Christ. I believe God can and will speak more details to different levels of ministry. While you may feel you have a specific word for a person that may be some- what controversial or private, it might not be your place to deliver such a word. If you truly feel God wants to give such a word, ask him to show you the right timing and method for delivery.

For example, Daniel had a difficult word to give King Nebuchadnezzar when God was warning him to humble himself, and Daniel could have railed against the king for his pride, declaring, "Thus says the Lord!" Daniel also could have been put to death right then and there. However, he instead spoke, "I wish the events foreshadowed in this dream would happen to your enemies, my lord, and not you!" (Daniel 4:19 NLT). Daniel not only heard from God, but he also used wisdom in how to deliver God's word to the king.

If God has given you a message to deliver to an in- dividual, speak clearly so that the individual can hear and understand you. In the excitement of the moment, you may be shouting, or crying, or speaking passionately, but if the person you are to "deliver the mail" to can't understand you, then you have not done your job. Remember that the purpose of ministry is to bring souls to Christ and glory to his name. There is more to ministering in the Spirit's gifts than simply moving in power. Maturity in the gifts means also moving in wisdom and love.

15

Manifestations

Emotions are a part of our makeup, and we all show our emotions in different manners. I believe this is also true concerning the way we express spiritual emotion, or how we display and demonstrate a manifestation of God in us. Upon feeling the presence and power of God, some cry, some shout, some dance, some fall under the power of God, while others tremble or simply smile—just to name a few.

We should be cautious in saying what is and what is not a manifestation of God in a person. God is the author of our faith—not us. As the author of both the person and the work he does in them, *he* determines what he will do as well as *how* he will do it and demonstrate it.

In John 9 we read of Jesus healing a man who was born blind. The Pharisees, upon hearing of the miracle and meeting the recipient of the miracle, criticized the miracle instead of celebrating it. Since they could not question the validity of the healing (it was obvious to all who knew the blind man since he had been born blind and could now see), rather than question the miracle, they questioned and nit-picked the methods used by the miracle worker, Jesus Christ:

> Then they took the man who had been blind to the Pharisees, because it was on the Sabbath that Jesus had made the mud and healed him. The Pharisees asked the man all about it. So he told them, "He put the mud over my eyes, and when I washed it away, I could see!" Some of the Pharisees said, "This man Jesus is not from God, for he is working on the Sabbath." Others said, "But how could an ordinary sinner do such miraculous signs?" So there was a deep division of opinion among them. (John 9:13–16 NLT)

Instead of focusing on the fact that Jesus had healed this man, their focus was on how and when Jesus had healed this man. How did he do it? When did he do it? What did he say? It is all too common for faith, healing, and miracle ministries to be criticized. Many times, they are not criticized for a lack of the supernatural but for the style of ministry—the things the prophet or minister may say, or the way in which he or she says it.

Once a man was ministering in a church camp meeting. The power of God moved in a very powerful and real way in each service. In one particular service, the presence of God was so strong that people began to fall all across the auditorium; they were slain in the Spirit. Almost everyone who was prayed for was slain in the Spirit. Others fell without anyone laying hands on them. The worship lasted for hours as people soaked in the glory of God.

After the service, one of the ministers in attendance invited the preacher of the camp meeting to minister to his church and said, "When you come to minister for me, I do not want anyone falling. None of that pushing people down business." I marvel that people have an issue with people being "slain in the Spirit," or that it would even be an issue in a Spirit-filled church. Were we not once called "holy rollers?" Our Pentecostal history tells us of people falling or being slain in the Spirit by the power of God. While on the floor, some began to roll. The Quakers quaked, the Methodists trembled, and the Pentecostals rolled. I'm not old enough to remember when this *did not* occur in our services and conventions. It has always happened throughout my entire life.

We read that Daniel heard the voice of God and had an encounter with an angel. The Bible says the following of his experience:

> As Gabriel approached the place where I was standing, I became so terrified that I fell with my face to the ground. "Son of man," he said, "you must understand that the events you have seen in your vision relate to the time of the end." While he was speaking, I fainted and lay there with my face to the ground. But Gabriel roused me with a touch and helped me to my feet. (Daniel 8:17–18 NLT)

John was slain in the presence of Jesus, as he wrote, "When I saw him, I fell at his feet as if I were dead. But he laid his right hand on me and said, 'Don't be afraid! I am the First and the Last'" (Revelation 1:17 NLT). Read what happened in the garden when the authorities arrived to arrest Jesus. Take note of the sixth verse:

> The leading priests and Pharisees had given Judas a contingent of Roman soldiers and Temple guards to accompany him. Now with blazing torches, lanterns, and weapons, they arrived at the olive grove. Jesus fully realized all that was going to happen to him, so he stepped forward to meet them. "Who are you looking for?" he asked. "Jesus the Nazarene," they replied. "I AM he," Jesus said. (Judas, who betrayed him, was standing with them.) *As Jesus said, "I AM he," they all drew back and fell to the ground!* (John 18:3–6 NLT, emphasis added)

You simply cannot put God in a box and treat the things of the Spirit as a science. I had one man tell me that if being slain in the Spirit is a work or manifestation of God, then the person must fall on their faces and not on their backs. It makes no difference if they fell on their backs or on their faces; the point is that they fell in the presence of God. The power of God was so strong, and the visitation too moving, and the word of God too powerful to stand, so they fell. Sometimes the power of God will knock you off your feet. I've given a few passages as evidence of individuals falling on their face and others falling back. In both instances, it was the work of God.

Within the Pentecostal/Charismatic movement we talk a lot of being "drunk in the Holy Spirit." When an officer suspects someone of drunk driving, they ask the driver to step out of their car and to walk a straight line. What is the purpose of the exercise? To see if the person stumbles and falls. Stumbling and falling is evidence of drunkenness.

Is this the only manifestation of the Holy Spirit? Of course not. Some dance and jump, some tremble in his presence, some have testified to feeling the warmth of the Holy Spirit in their bodies, others feel a chill, some laugh, and some cry. One thing is for certain: After you have been in the presence of God, your soul will thirst to praise him, and you will be in awe of his glory. When he shows up, he will manifest his power. Seek the manifestation of God's power.

16

Use Me, Lord!

The people of Israel willingly accepted the invitation to Mount Carmel to witness the showdown between the prophets of Baal and the Prophet Elijah. They went anxiously and expectant to see something.

When the prophets of Baal failed to produce a supernatural manifestation of fire falling from heaven, Elijah called the people to gather around him. The Bible says, "They all crowded around him" (1 Kings 18:30 NLT). Humanity is hungry for the supernatural. There is a fascination and curiosity for the supernatural. Without question, this world wants to see, feel, and experience something. Man's religions have failed time and again, false gods will continue to remain silent, their philosophers will continue to argue and never find absolute truth.

What about us? What will we do? We must be ready!

God has positioned us as he did with the prophet Elijah on Mount Carmel, so that the eyes of the world can see the marvelous and mighty works of the Holy One of Israel through us. I believe the Lord will position you to show his glory. It might be at your workplace, in a church service, on an airplane, among leaders of men, women, and world leaders. Be ready!

Be ready to be a vessel of God and to demonstrate the mighty power of God in your world. When you hear others say their gods and philosophies have failed them, when self-help was no help at all, when you see them seeking for something more, be ready for your Elijah moment.

I want to be ready. I want to be positioned. I want to demonstrate the power of our God! I want the world to know and proclaim with me, "Hear, O Israel, the Lord our God is one Lord!" It is our mission to let the world know there is no other God but the Holy One of Israel. I want humanity to witness through us that all power, glory, praise, and honor belong to him.

The Church Stands Triumphant!

According to the critics and doomsday false prophets, we should not even be here. They have falsely predicted the falling of the Christian church for centuries. In 1917, communist officials declared in Russia that by dawn of the twenty-first century the entire world would embrace Communism, and Christianity would be eradicated from the earth. In the 1930s, the Nazi regime proclaimed they would outlast the followers of Jesus. In the 1960s, a world-famous band declared, "We're more popular than Jesus." The attacks and false prophecies and mockeries have not ceased. Think of Osama bin Laden's attacks on 9/11, or even the popular, American comic who spoke despairingly of Jesus in an acceptance speech by saying, "This award is my god now."

We have those who have tried to remove "In God We Trust" from our currency and "One nation under God" from our pledge. Several groups are on a mission to remove all resemblance of the Judeo-Christian values that are embedded in the foundation of our nation. These things should not alarm us. It was foretold by Christ, "The kingdom of heaven suffers violence" (Matthew 11:12).

The communists and the Nazis prophesied that Christianity would die by the turn of the twentieth century. Well, here we are! Lenin is entombed, and the Third Reich is gone. But the church of the Living God continues on in victory! After the attacks, the criticism, the division, and the schisms, they must ask, "How can the church still stand?"

Our Foundation Is Jesus Christ

The church stands because of what it stands upon. If we stood on philosophers, we would crumble as the Greek empire did. If we were built on a political platform, we would crumble as the Roman Empire did. If we stood on barbarianism, we would become extinct as the Vikings did.

We do not stand on any of those things, but we stand on an unmovable, unshakeable, unchangeable, incomparable foundation that is rock solid. This foundation is not an "it"; it is a "he."

He has become the chief cornerstone.

He is the stone that the builders rejected.

He has a name. The church still stands because it is built on Jesus Christ the solid rock. Once we understand that Jesus is the captain of this ship—the Lord of the harvest, the head of the church—*then* activation and emancipation can come.

This modern generation has battled insecurity and understanding what and where their place is. We try to find ourselves in our roots, race, and culture. We seek affirmation from our social circles or from a checklist found in a book. While our culture, race, roots, family lineage, and history all play a part in making us who we are, our identity is not found in those areas. Your identity is not found in those areas. Your identity is found in Christ!

Mark 4 tells the story of Jesus and his disciples in a boat. The storm came, the winds blew, the seas raged, the rain fell, and fear came among them. In the midst of all of that, Jesus was found lying on a pillow taking a nap. After being awoken by these concerned men, Jesus rebuked the winds and the storm by saying, "Peace! Be still!" (v. 39).

It was by Jesus' spoken word that the winds, seas, storms, and waves came into being, so when Jesus spoke, all these things recognized and obeyed the voice of the Creator. The winds and storm ceased, and the sea was calm. Rather than Simon giving Andrew or John a high five, the followers of Jesus—with bewildered looks and frightened and confused minds asked, "Who then is this, that even the wind and the sea obey him?" (v. 41).

They walked with him and talked with him. They saw him perform miracles, heard him speak to others, and even more incredibly, they worked for him, yet they did not know him for themselves. They lacked revelation of whom they were following. Up until now he was a rabbi, a good teacher, someone interesting, but now they began to wonder. They realized he was no mere teacher; he was the Son of God, the Messiah, the one sure and everlasting foundation.

It's Not Just Our Legacy—It's Our Commission

The following verses have been recited and preached so many times that most of us know them by memory:

> "John baptized with water, but in just a few days you will be baptized with the Holy Spirit ... But you will receive power when the Holy Spirit comes upon you. And you will be my witnesses, telling people about me everywhere—in Jerusalem, throughout Judea, in Samaria, and to the ends of the earth." (Acts 1:5,8 NLT)

> "No, what you see was predicted long ago by the prophet Joel: 'In the last days,' God says, 'I will pour out my Spirit upon all people. Your sons and daughters will prophesy. Your young men will see visions, and your old men will dream dreams. In those days I will pour out my Spirit even on my servants— men and women alike—and they will prophesy.'" (Acts 2:16–18 NLT)

"These miraculous signs will accompany those who believe: They will cast out demons in my name, and they will speak in new languages. They will be able to handle snakes with safety, and if they drink anything poisonous, it won't hurt them. They will be able to place their hands on the sick, and they will be healed." (Mark 16:17–18 NLT)

"Truly, I say to you, whatever you bind on earth shall be bound in heaven, and whatever you loose on earth shall be loosed in heaven. Again I say to you, if two of you agree on earth about anything they ask, it will be done for them by my Father in heaven. For where two or three are gathered in my name, there am I among them." (Matthew 18:18–20)

"The Spirit of the Lord is upon me, because he has anointed me to proclaim good news to the poor. He has sent me to proclaim liberty to the captives and recovering of sight to the blind, to set at liberty those who are oppressed, to proclaim the year of the Lord's favor." (Luke 4:18–19)

We have sung about those verses, we have celebrated

them, we have danced to them, and we have "shouted the house down" about them. I could walk into almost any Spirit-filled church and say any of those verses and guarantee you that I'd be hearing several people declare, "Amen!" And that's good. It is worth shouting about. God chose us to be the temple of the Holy Spirit, and it is cause for celebration.

That is our heritage. This is what sets us apart from the rest of the Evangelical movement. While some sing about how God's Spirit moved about the face of the waters, we sing about a God who has moved in us and taken up residence in our hearts. We must grasp, as those who are living and writing the twenty-ninth chapter of Acts, that these verses were not written just to sing about or dance about; they were written to tell us what we have at our disposal for the task at hand.

Those verses weren't written to inspire us for a good choir song, but to tell us what we are armed with and what is at our disposal through the power of the Holy Spirit. These verses are directly connected to the commandment of Jesus when He said:

> "Go into all the world and proclaim the gospel to the whole creation." (Mark 16:15)

> "I have been given all authority in heaven and on earth. Therefore, go and make disciples of all the nations, baptizing them in the name of the Father and the Son and the Holy Spirit." (Matthew 28:18–19 NLT)

What a shame it would be for us to have so much power bottled up inside of us and not use it. The baptism of the Holy Spirit was an empowerment, so that you and I could write that next chapter, continue doing God's work on the earth, and shine the light of Christ so that the increase of the kingdom of God would have no end.

The verses I referenced convict me. They tell me of how much God has given. They tell me about my potential and my abilities. The reason they convict me is because they leave me no excuses. I can't go to God and say, "Lord, I couldn't reach someone with the gospel because I didn't have any strength to do it. I didn't have the words to say." I can't tell Jesus, "Lord, I was going to pray for that individual who was ill, but I didn't know if you would listen to my prayers." I have no excuses.

I don't want it to be said that God sent someone to share the gospel with you and me, but he couldn't get you and me to reach for someone else to share his good news with them. I have to continually ask myself, *What am I doing with my anointing? What am I doing with the talent God gave me? What have I done to share my testimony? What am I doing to reflect Christ to those who are around me?*

A man once told me we are all missionaries. Your mission field is the space between your two feet and wherever you walk. There is no higher or greater calling than to be called into the service of the King. We all have different capacities and abilities within the body of Christ, but it is the same Spirit who brought us all together.

Never Underestimate Your Testimony

Probably the greatest tool you have to reach someone (outside of the unction of the Holy Spirit) is your personal testimony. If all you do is tell people about Daniel and the lion's den and Noah and the ark, they may not be able to relate to those stories. But when you open up and share what God did for you, all of a sudden God becomes relevant to them.

More than that, your testimony releases the power of God into their life. Is your testimony that you were saved from drugs? Were you a prodigal who came home? Were you saved from religious works into knowing the power of God for salvation? Find the people who need your testimony, ask God to bring you across their path, and share your testimony boldly. Your words have the power to release the same work of God into their lives.

Your greatest testimony is your salvation testimony—even if you never wandered from the Lord and have loved him all your life. This will always be the greatest miracle you can experience. But that is not the only work God has done in your life. What else have you seen God do for you? Did he come through with miraculous provision? Has he enabled you to have children after you were declared barren? Were you healed of disease or infirmity? Did his word set you free from hopelessness and depression? Has he saved you from insecurities and fears and given you confidence in who you are in him? These are your testimonies! You overcome with the power of your testimony, and through your testimony, others will receive their miracle in Jesus' name and learn to overcome, too.

The price for the salvation of souls was blood from the spotless Lamb of God. He paid a high price for souls, and I can't turn my back to the world and *not* try to reach them. I can't be so "holier than thou" that when I walk in the mall and see all these "sinners" around me and think they'll never change. Such were some of us, but someone thought you were worth sharing the gospel with. The salvation of souls caused God to manifest in the flesh and bear our sin on a cross. Salvation was expensive to God, but he thought you and I were worth it.

There was a season of my life where I made a living selling cars. I still remember how people used to get insulted when they wanted to trade in their car. In their minds, their car was always worth a certain amount of dollars; however, my appraiser thought their car was worth a different amount.

There'd come a point in the argument where we'd finally have to say, "Look, you may think your car is worth that much, but this is all we can give you for it. If you think you can get more, sell it on your own." More often than not, after a few weeks and after money was spent on advertisements the paper and in auto magazines, the individual would return to accept the deal we originally offered.

You see, things are really only worth what someone will pay for them. You can have a baseball card, an autograph, a car, a diamond, a painting—anything, and you can tell everyone, "This is worth this much!" But that may not be true. What you should say is, "This is its estimated value" or "This is how much I think it's worth," because until someone pays for it, it's just hypothetical. Things are only worth what someone is willing to pay for them. When God looked through eternity and saw all of us, he thought we were worth his blood and his life. God loved the world enough to give his best and equip us to tell the world the story of the best gift the world has ever known.

The promise of the Father that the apostles so earnestly waited for was never to be a one-time event, but this promise is unto you and your children and your children's children and all who are far off—including you and me.

This Promise Is Still Accessible Today

God still wants to pour out his Spirit just as it was prophesied by Joel and just as it was confirmed by Peter. If you have never been baptized in the Holy Spirit, prepare and wait on the Lord for it. This promise is for you! For those who are reading this and who have already been baptized in power, let us pray for a fresh outpouring that renews our passion and zeal to make Jesus famous throughout the earth.

Pentecost, or Shavuot, was also known in the Bible as the Feast of Harvest. Celebrated on the fiftieth day after Passover, Shavuot is traditionally a joyous time of giving thanks and presenting offerings for the new grain of the summer wheat harvest in Israel.[4] The name "Feast of Weeks" was given to the feast of Pentecost because God commanded the Jews in Leviticus 23:15–16 to count seven full weeks (or forty-nine days), beginning on the second day of Passover, and then present offerings of new grain to the Lord.[5]

Shavuot was originally a festival for expressing thankfulness to the Lord for the blessing of the harvest,[6] but the celebration is also tied to the giving of the Ten Commandments.[7] Jews believe that it was at exactly this time that Moses went up the mountain, and God gave the Torah to the people through Moses on Mount Sinai.[8]

When the promise of the Father descended on the upper room, as described in Acts 2, believers joined together as once again Pentecost, or Shavuot, became a day to thank God for a harvest, and a harvest immediately happened. When a crowd gathered to see what the commotion caused by the Holy Spirit was, Peter preached a message that led three thousand souls to be harvested into God's kingdom. The feast of Pentecost, as they celebrated it under the law, was a type and foreshadow of what would happen in the New Testament. When Moses went up to Mount Sinai to wait on the Lord, the word of God was given to the Israelites at Shavuot. When the Jews accepted the Torah, they became servants of God.

Similarly, after Jesus went up to heaven, the Holy Spirit was given at Pentecost. When the disciples received the gift, they became witnesses for Christ. Jews celebrated a joyous harvest on Shavuot, and the church celebrated a harvest of newborn souls on Pentecost. The disciples went to the upper room, received the Holy Spirit, and then brought down that same Spirit to the people. The day that we are living in is a day of thanksgiving; there's another harvest in front of us.

At the onset of this year, I felt the Holy Spirit quicken my spirit with the following word: "Tell my people that if they will release the sound of Pentecost, I will release the power of Pentecost." Acts 2 says that when the day of Pentecost was fully come, there was a sound of a mighty rushing wind that filled the house where they were sitting. Where did the sound come from? There are no actual sounds in wind or air; the sound comes from whatever the air or wind touches as it passes through.

The sound of the mighty rushing wind was produced when heaven touched earth. Something celestial touched something mortal, and heaven crossed into our atmosphere, creating a sound that came forth from the one hundred and twenty faithful individuals in the upper room. The sound of the one hundred and twenty caused the sound of three thousand more faithful to be added within a day, and millions upon millions more today.

17

The Cause of the Gospel

There is a price to pay for serving the Lord. Surely, the price is greater for some of us than it is for others. I recall Bishop G.E. Patterson, the great presiding bishop of the Church of God in Christ, saying in a sermon, "Salvation is free, but it's not cheap."

Missionaries and Evangelists

In 1956 a group of American missionaries set off to the jungle in Ecuador to introduce Jesus Christ to an indigenous tribe in the Amazons. It was there that Nate Saint, Jim Elliot, Peter Fleming, Ed McCully, and Roger Youderian were murdered at the end of the spear. As someone who has experienced substantial loss, I know their pain. I know the despair, anger, and confusion their widows and children must have felt. Everyone would have understood if these families had grown bitter. Surely, the widows and children left Ecuador, returned to the States, and never thought about missions work again. Surely, there would be a root of bitterness against those who had killed their family members. Yet these families, consumed with fiery passion to make Jesus famous, did exactly the opposite.

The words of the slain missionary, Jim Elliot, went from simply being the personal reflections in a journal to a prophetic mandate and spiritual calling for his family. Inside his journal, they found the following verse written: Luke 9:24: "For whosoever will save his life shall lose it: but whosoever will lose his life for my sake, the same shall save it" (KJV). Jim followed that passage with these words: "He is no fool who gives what he cannot keep to gain what he cannot lose."

Jim Elliot's widow, Elisabeth, and Nate Saint's sister, Rachel, kept preaching. They kept sharing the name of Jesus. They didn't leave; they stayed, and they kept sharing the call that was on their lives. Eventually, Rachel led the same indigenous tribe that had killed Nate to the saving knowledge of the Lord Jesus Christ. Hell should have won the battle in Ecuador, but the gates of hell did not prevail. Hell should have won the battle in the Amazons, but the gates of hell did not prevail. Surely hell should have overcome the families of these slain missionaries, yet even amidst murder, deceit, grief, and sorrow, the gates of hell did not prevail.

Colombia

My paternal family hails from the country of Colombia on the continent of South America, which experienced a great revival in the early twentieth century. Revival spread quickly throughout the country as many came to the knowledge of Jesus Christ, so much so that it caught the attention of the government.

The president at the time was committed to eradicating the Protestant movement from the country of Colombia. It was common for churches to be destroyed and for preachers to be killed. Our own family suffered great persecution. I recall stories my grandparents told me about bombs that were thrown through the windows of their churches, poison that was dumped into their water wells, and rocks that were thrown at them, but the gates of hell did not prevail.

My father would often stand on a street corner in Colombia with a guitar strapped around him, and he would sing songs unto the Lord and preach the gospel of Jesus Christ. One day while doing so, a government-sanctioned gang instructed to silence the Protestant church began throwing rocks at him. Hitting him in his head and aiming for his eyes, they eventually rendered him unconscious and bloody on the street corner. Committed to his life's calling, when he awoke from his unconscious state, my father cleaned himself off and continued preaching the gospel on that street corner because the gates of hell cannot prevail.

My grandfather told me the story of the poisoning of their water well. Their neighbor, Don Tulio, was tired of living next to evangelicals, and he was determined to kill my grandparents. Rather than fall ill from the poison, my family showed signs of strength and perfect health. They were like Daniel inside the courts of Nebuchadnezzar. Many days later, my grandfather heard a knock at the door. When he opened the door, Don Tulio was on his knees. He said, "I've tried to kill you, but rather than die, you have life. I don't know what you have, but I want what you have." Don Tulio gave his life to the Lord Jesus Christ on that doorstep, and he repented of his sins. Not only did God save Don Tulio, but Don Tulio also became an ordained minister, pastor, preacher, and evangelist of the gospel of Lord Jesus Christ. Don Tulio was eventually killed for his faith. He was a modern-day martyr for the cause of the gospel, and one more time, the gates of hell did not prevail.

Witch doctors once came to our home and tried to curse my father and my uncle. They tried to cause them harm and stop them from preaching the gospel. The witch doctors sang their chants and attempted to silence the men of God, yet my uncle raised his voice and prayed against them. He said, "In the name of Jesus, you will not speak, and you will not move until we are done." Those witch doctors were virtually frozen in place and did not speak and did not move. They were held by the power of God, so that they could not hinder the preaching of the gospel. They were unable to move until my father and my uncle finished the message and the call to salvation.

My father went to be with Lord, and the only thing that man cared about was preaching Jesus. It's the only thing he cared that his kids did. It's the only thing he cared that his grandchildren did. My grandfather died at the age of ninety-one, and he never stopped preaching the gospel. My grandmother is a strong woman, but she would sometimes act like she was frail. She would wobble onto a bus, and once the bus driver closed door, she'd turn around, point her finger at the other passengers, and say, "Repent, you generation of vipers!" She'd start preaching the gospel. The gospel is the only thing I've ever known in my life. All the good that I've ever experienced has been in the church. All the bad I've ever experienced has also been in the church, but I haven't given up on it.

The Church Has Persevered

I could tell many stories of what God did in my family. Colombia, a country full of persecution, soon became the epicenter for the church in South America. Not only did they experience revival, but they also sent thousands of missionaries to countries around the world. Similar stories can be told from each nation to which the gospel has already been preached. From the deserts and jungles of Africa, to the forests of Asia, the underground in China, and inside the caves of the Middle East—the church has persevered, and the gates of hell have not prevailed.

Decades of communism have not been able to stop the gospel from spreading in China. After the Cultural Revolution in China, some people estimated that there were no Christians left in the entire nation. They knew all the foreign missionaries had been driven out and had heard stories of the Chinese believers who were being imprisoned and killed. The communists left no stone unturned in their work to stamp out the light of the gospel. Now, an estimated 105 million believers in China still declare that Jesus Christ is the son of the living God.[9] Those are just our estimates, and they don't even account for those whom we have yet to find. We thought we were going to find a defeated church, but we found a triumphant church.

Thousands of years of battle against Christianity have not been able to prevent the Word from reaching the Islamic regions of the world. When missionaries went into Afghanistan and back into Iraq, we thought we were going to have to start all over again. But in the caves of Afghanistan and Iraq, we found believers who were still worshiping, glorifying, and lifting up the name of the Lord Jesus Christ.

I suspect that one day, when the door to North Korea is finally opened, we're going to find a remnant of Christians who still worship the Lord Jesus Christ. They've suffered persecution, trial, and strife, but they will count decades of persecution as gain because their testimonies will be that they did it all for the cause of the gospel of the Lord Jesus Christ.

I have heard countless stories of men and women who have preached this gospel and witnessed God show mighty signs and wonders as a way of proving to his children that he is the One, the true, and the living God. Missionaries and modern-day martyrs have laid down their lives. The price paid by these heroes of our faith have been great, but they counted it all worthy for the cause of establishing the church and preaching the name of Jesus.

God Trusts Us with His Church

Despite the efforts that have been made to stamp out our influence, and despite wars that have been raged against our faith, God still trusts us with his church. We deal with a lot of trust issues toward him, but I'm here to declare that God trusts us. He trusts you with his church. How do I know it? Because he hasn't taken it away from us yet.

Think of how many times the media has said the church is on a downward spiral, and we're bound to go under. It doesn't matter what media group you like; it doesn't matter what station you tune into. We've been hearing for years now that the church is on the decline.

Pastor Rod Parsley recently spoke of the overwhelming number of people coming to Christ in churches two years old or newer. Since these are church plants that typically don't have their own building yet, these new believers are coming to faith in gymnasiums, storefronts, discipleship groups, life classes, and the like. Where faith happens is not nearly as significant as that it happens.

Billions of people have come and continue to come to the knowledge that Jesus Christ is the same yesterday, today, and forever. This kind of movement only happens if you are commissioned of God, anointed of the Holy Spirit, and full of the power that is in the name of Jesus.

If God trusts us that much with his church, I pray that all insecurity comes off us. I pray that all negative spirits come off us. I pray all pessimism leaves us, and I pray we thank God for his church and feel proud to be a part of it— so proud that we share the good news of the gospel of Jesus Christ with every person with whom we come in contact.

God's trusting of us with his church is further confirmation that the gates of hell did not prevail in the first century, or the second century, or any time since, and if it didn't prevail for the last twenty centuries, it's not going to prevail in the twenty-first century. We are the triumphant, glorious church of which God said there shall be no end. God trusts us with his church, and I've never been more excited to be a part of it.

18

Acts 29

The church has been mired in controversy since its inception, yet we've been able to advance the gospel and make disciples anyway. Look at how we've persevered! Look at how we've grown and how God has blessed us!

After all my reading and rereading of the book of Acts, it became clear: I do want a book-of-Acts church. I want to be the church that survives despite trial and tribulation, fighting and scandal, all while guiding thousands upon thousands to the saving knowledge of the Lord Jesus Christ. The greatest promise we have as a church is that despite every problem we have had, the gates of hell have not prevailed against the church.

To see, know, and understand our shortcomings and weaknesses is, in itself, a testimony to the power of the gospel of Jesus Christ. What promising news it is to us that God has used and continues to use broken vessels for his glory! God makes himself perfect inside and through his imperfect church. It's been over two thousand years and the church is still making disciples. The church is still going, and it keeps growing. It's still endued with power. Thousands of believers continue to come to Christ.

I used to host a conference called Acts 29. The premise was to open believers to the revelation that through our words, deeds, and actions, we are writing the next chapter—you and I—through the power of the Holy Spirit and for the glory of Christ. God appointed you and I to be the twenty-ninth chapter of Acts. It's the only book in the Bible that doesn't have an ending. It is surely the to-be-continued book of the Bible.

As we celebrate the keeping power of his church, we are also desperately aware and convicted that after thousands of years, hundreds of translations of the Bible, and all the tremendous work that's been done for the cause of Christ and his namesake, there are still approximately 1,600 language groups that don't have any portion of the Bible translated in their native language, and another 2,500 are only in process of translating the Bible.[10] That's four thousand language groups who still don't know that there's only one name given unto men by which we can be saved (Acts 4:12).

Unto All Nations

While I admit I'm not an ardent student of eschatology, I know enough to understand that Jesus is coming. The signs of the times confirm that fact. As someone who has heard that Jesus is coming for as far back as I can remember, I admit that at times I've been perplexed by why he hasn't come just yet. I think I've found the answer in a commonly known verse that I've read time and again, yet it stood out to me just a few years ago: "And this gospel of the kingdom shall be preached in all the world for a witness unto all nations; and then shall the end come" (Matthew 24:14 HCSB).

The end of times cannot come until these language groups receive the gospel and have the opportunity to hear the blessed name of the Messiah, the Son of the living God, and have the opportunity to call on his saving name. Pastor Samuel Rodriguez captured my heart when he so emphatically declared, "The church is waiting for Jesus to come down, and Jesus is waiting for the church to rise up!" We are to rise up and preach. We are to rise up and make disciples, to rise up and operate in the gifts of the spirit, to rise up and make Jesus known. We've heard so many preachers say it, and I wish I had said it first, "You're waiting for God, but God's waiting for you."

The Bible says that when this gospel is preached to everyone, when it reaches the ends of the earth, then the end will come. People so often look up to the moon—red moons, and blood moons—for the signs of the end of times. But the true sign is when this gospel is preached to every creature. I believe with all of my heart that the merciful hand of Jesus is covering the bell of Gabriel's rapture trumpet and by doing so delaying the cue to the archangel to sound the trumpet of rescue, so that these language groups—and your family members and friends who have not yet heard that God so loved them that he gave his only begotten Son, so that whoever believes in him will not perish but have everlasting life—would have that opportunity. The only thing standing between us and the second coming of the Lord Jesus Christ is the triumphant church's ability to continue to triumph, preach, teach, and make disciples.

We are to keep writing the story and to keep showing the gospel and its marvelous light, its signs, its miracles, and its wonders. The church keeps triumphing because we are the triumphant church. We go from glory to glory to glory. We go from victory to victory to victory. After every glory, and after every victory, it's shown again and again: The gates of hell cannot prevail against the triumphant church of the Lord Jesus Christ.

Passing the Torch to Every Generation

I'm an old soul. I like old music, and I live in nostalgia sometimes. I have jokingly told the Lord, "God, when we get to heaven, can we have a time machine? Because I'd love to go back to the healing revivals of the thirties, forties, and fifties and be around the voices of the revival and see those like A. A. Allen in their prime. I'd love to see Oral Roberts when he was thirty years old and preaching in tents. I'd love to see when Billy Graham and Oral Roberts broke down the color barrier by dismantling the rope that divided the races and said, "No longer do whites sit here, and African Americans sit there."

I would love to see those days, and I told the Lord, "When we get to heaven, it's eternity; I mean we have a while up there. Could I borrow a time machine and just go back? I want to see what it was like. And at times, feeling like an old soul, I ask God, "Why didn't you let me be born in the fifties or the sixties, or even a little earlier?" I would have loved to be in those times. And the Lord said, "I put you where you are to carry the flag, the torch, that your father, your grandparents, and your great-grandparents passed down to you, so that there would be a witness in every generation."

Perfectly Matched

You and I are perfectly matched, perfectly fitted to the twenty-first century church. He could have given the last-day church to anybody. He could have given it to Smith Wigglesworth, or Oral Roberts. He could have given it to the "ABC's" of the Voice of Healing movement or the likes of Kathryn Kuhlman. He could have given it to any general of the faith, but he trusted you and I to be the glorious church of the last day. He trusts you and I to finish the race with excellence, triumph, and victory.

I don't believe Jesus is coming back for a church that's defeated or smaller than when he left. He's not coming back as the lamb of God or as the babe in the manger. When that trumpet sounds, and Jesus lifts his hand of mercy off the bell of Gabriel's trumpet and says, "Sound the alarm," when that glorious, beautiful, triumphant day comes, he's coming back as the Lion of the tribe of Judah to reign as the King of kings and the Lord of lords.

I don't think our best days are behind us; I think our greatest days are in front of us. Before the history of humankind is over and done with, we're going to see every word accomplished. We're going to see every promise fulfilled. We're going to see every prophetic word come to pass.

This world will know; heaven will know, and everything under the earth will know there's no God like Jehovah. There's no name like Jesus, and the gates of hell cannot prevail against the body of Christ.

The body of Christ was broken one time, but it wasn't for defeat. It was broken for victory because the moment it was broken, I was saved, you were saved, I was healed, and you were healed, and from that time forward, the gates of hell shall not prevail against the church. He will come back to celebrate that we are a triumphant, victorious, glorious church of which the gates of hell have not been able to prevail against.

The Triumphant Church

The triumphant church is precisely who we are. In Christ we have won the battle. We are victorious! And because of the cross of Calvary, we rejoice with great jubilation. This is the church of Jesus Christ of which you and I are a part—from the time of the tomb to our present day.

Before Israel took the city of Jericho, there was a "shout" that came forth. Before the Holy Spirit fell, there was a sound of a mighty rushing wind that filled the house. We are the ones to raise up the sound again, to cry out and shout to be filled again with a fresh Pentecost infilling and outpouring of the Holy Spirit. He fills us, he empowers us, and he releases us into the fields of harvest. The fields are white with ripeness, if we will just go out to them as God's triumphant church. That's why I am declaring to you today with great confidence that we are about to have a harvest of souls. We are about to be blessed with the Holy Spirit like never before.

> Father, I thank you today for being a part of the church of the Lord Jesus Christ. I want to thank you, God, that you chose us because you didn't have to, but you grafted us into the family. You made us joint heirs with Christ. I want to thank you today that you trusted us enough to believe that we could lead and be participants in this latter-day revival and in this last-day church. Father, all the signs point to your coming. I believe you're coming again, and I believe it's very soon.

The *Triumphant Church* is simply my sound to my generation that the gates of hell will not prevail against us. The church will live, victory is ours, and soon all the world will know Jesus is Lord! *I thank you God, that we're part of finishing the race. I thank you that we're part of running the race with victory, with glory, and with triumph.* I can't wait to get to heaven. I can't wait to see the generals of the faith gather and say, "Lord, look what we've done in your name. Look at the souls we have won. Look at those who have been discipled." And I can't wait to hear the Father's voice say, "Well done, perfect servants."

Notes

[1]Gloria Gaither, *Something Beautiful: The Stories behind a Half-Century of the Songs of Bill and Gloria Gaither* (New York: FaithWords, 2007), n.p.

[2]Glenn T. Stanton, "New Harvard Research Says U.S. Christianity Is Not Shrinking, But Growing Stronger," *The Federalist*, January 22, 2018, http://thefederalist.com/2018/01/22/new-harvard-research-says-u-s-christianity-not-shrinking-growing-stronger.

[3]Aleksandra Sandstrom and Becka A. Alper, "Church Involvement Varies Widely among U.S. Christians," Pew Research Center, November 16, 2015, http://www.pewresearch.org/fact-tank/2015/11/16/church-involvement-varies-widely-among-u-s-christians.

[4]Mary Fairchild, "Passover Feast for Christians," *ThoughtCo.*, April 23, 2018, https://www.thoughtco.com/bible-feast-of-passover-700185.

[5]Mary Fairchild, "Introduction to the Book of Leviticus," *ThoughtCo.*, August 13, 2018, https://www.thoughtco.com/book-of-leviticus-701146.

[6]Ariela Pelaia, "What Is Shavuot?," *ThoughtCo.*, July 28, 2017, https://www.thoughtco.com/what-is-shavuot-2076487.

[7]Mary Fairchild, "What Are the Ten Commandments?," *ThoughtCo.*, January 26, 2018, https://www.thoughtco.com/ten-commandments-p2-700221.

[8]Jack Zavada, "Moses—Giver of the Law," *ThoughtCo.*, August 17, 2017, https://www.thoughtco.com/moses-giver-of-the-law-701173.

[9]Operation World, "China: People's Republic of China," http://www.operationworld.org/country/chna/owtext.html.

[10]Wycliffe, "Why Bible Translation?," https://www.wycliffe.org/about/why.

About the Author

Tony Suárez is an author, sought-after speaker, and pastor. He serves as the executive vice president of the National Hispanic Christian Leadership Conference (NHCLC), the country's largest Hispanic Evangelical organization, serving more than forty thousand congregations in the United States.

Suárez regularly conducts evangelistic and healing services overseas and speaks at churches, conferences, and various events weekly across the United States. Through his role as executive vice president and head of the NHCLC's Washington, DC, office, Suárez has become an active member of the Washington, DC, community, where he serves as a member of the President's evangelical advisory board, regularly meets with members of the House of Representatives and the Senate, and speaks at events where the voice and participation of the NHCLC has been requested.

Newsmax has named Suárez as one of the fifty most influential Republican Latinos in the United States. He has become a prominent voice within the Evangelical community, a trusted guest speaker, and a sought-after media resource (featured on CNN, TBN, MSNBC, Telemundo,

Univision, Mundo Fox, NBC Latino, WGN, CBN, *Charisma*, and *The Christian Post*, to name a few). He is a regular host on TBN, and his television program, *Faith Alive*, can be seen daily on TBN Salsa. Suárez also serves on various committees, including the Faith Advisory Board for the White House, the American Heart Association Diversity Council, Hispanic Israel Leadership Council (HILC), Bible Study Fellowship, and Una Familia Foundation. He was also selected as one of the top ten candidates for the 2016 John C. Maxwell Leadership Award.

Prior to his work with NHCLC, he founded The Pentecostals of Norfolk Church in Virginia in 2007, where he served as senior pastor until 2013. During his pastorate, Suárez founded The Norfolk Learning Center in collaboration with Regent University's Youth and Urban Renewal Center. Tony is most proud of being the father of three amazing children.